SPEAKPUBLISHING books are available at quantity discounts with bulk purchase for educational, business, churches or sales promotional use. For information please send an email to speakpubone@gmail.com with subject: Bulk ordering.
Cover Design By: Darell Threeths
Darell Threeths has single handedly designed each cover in the Beautifully Ugly People! Series. He has Studied Fine Arts at Florida A&M University and is currently pursuing his dreams in art as he resides in Boca Raton, Fl. You can find out more about him and his art work here at http://www.facebook.com/threethsartmusic

Third Edition December 2020
Published Digitally and Printed in the United States of America.

I0108300

Book#3 of 'BEAUTIFULLY UGLY PEOPLE' SERIES

MORE BEAUTI- FULLY UGLY PEOPLE!

Michael D. Beckford

"Reeling In One Reader At A Time."

A Michael Beckford Group LLC Subsidiary.

MORE BEAUTIFULLY UGLY PEOPLE

Isbn-10: 0-9824189-1-4
Isbn-13: 978-0-9824189-1-8
SPEAKPUBLISHING BOOKS EDITION
Attention: Schools, Churches, Corporations and Non-Profit Businesses.

DEDICATION PAGE

I dedicate this book to my Lord and Savior Jesus Christ. Lord you are good and your mercies endure forever. I may not be a perfect writer, but at least I know that I serve a perfect God.

POSSESSED

Have you ever woken up in the morning and felt like you didn't belong? You looked in the mirror at your life and said, "God, why are these people so crazy?" As Pastor Hall does another one of his casting out demons, I begin to wonder what my brother is doing up at Clark Atlanta University. It's been five years since my mother and father decided to get hitched again, and those two can't stop smooching each other. It's also been two years since I hit full blown puberty. Now I'm seventeen, and my parents are talking about casting the devil or legions out of me. Why? I'm a good girl; I'm just going through a few things, natural things that exist in all who live to see the years of their teens.

I'm seventeen now, and most likely, they still think of me as "Little Precious," but I'm far from that "Little Precious" title. Just call me Precious, and you and I will be just fine.

There he goes again, Pastor Hall screaming

out the name of the Father, of the Son, and of the Holy Ghost. Somebody please get a bucket, because this lady is sure to throw up. She's possessed with demons, alright. It looks more like she's getting rid of a Snickers bar. Demons, demons, demons; everyone seems to be scared of these demons. I'm not afraid of them; they are so 1970s. For the sake of peace, I just shake my head up and down like a bobble head doll every time my mother brings up the subject. Yuck! Yuck, the lady is barfing all over the place. Pastor Hall, leave her alone! Pretty soon the whole church is going to puke. Then yes, we will be a demon free church.   Looks like he's finally ready to speak and handle his real pastoral duties. Nobody told him to start performing exorcisms; this man has got to be crazy. I hope the rest of his message is short and sweet. I don't have time for no long-winded, demon-casting, oil-throwing, breath-smelling, cross-bearing sermon.

Here he comes to the podium, with his two gold teeth on the front of his top grill, looking like Bugs Bunny over a hot Sunday dinner. Why does a fifty-something year-old pastor need brand new gold teeth? Scratch that. He doesn't look like Bugs Bunny; he looks like Rev. Thug with his deathly jet black suit, gold plated cross and alligators slipped on his feet straight from the Everglades. Let me stop judging Pastor Hall. He's been good to my family for years. Maybe he's just a little out of touch, or maybe he's just a little cute in his own way.

"Come, come all ye that labor, and I will give you rest. Come to me all you who are weary, all who have been struggling with the demons which possess your soul."

Pastor Hall drizzled out the few words with the little energy he could muster. I guess he is trying to get some more victims to come forward and be cast out. That's funny. Cast out. It sounds like the prescription for a detoxification, when people try to lose all that weight, and they use the bathroom everywhere. I don't know; I just get a creepy feeling inside when people talk about casting out and detoxifying. All of it is just extremely gross.

What the heck is going on here at First Baptist Church of Tallahassee? Somebody done brought hell in here, and Pastor Hall is trying hard to get it out. If I knew it was going to be a detoxification party in here today I would have brought my shades. I don't have time for no funny spirits looking at me. I'm too cute for that.   There he goes again. Wow! Look at that lady. That's an old soul being purged. Oh no, she's talking like a man. Ok, I am officially terrified. This is not funny anymore. Jesus help me. Help me Lord Jesus. Oh no, not the twisting of the head lady, and this is supposed to be one of the mothers of the church who sits to the front. I didn't know that those old ladies with the long hats on could be possessed by demons; I thought that them long hats and long white dresses shielded them from the mastery of the devils troops, better known as demons.

"Come, yes, come forward. God wants to heal you; he wants to purge you. Let him purify your life, body, soul, and mind. Would you come?" Pastor Hall I think you need to stop. How many of them jokers are you trying to slay for today. Save some oil for later. Oils are expensive these days, especially peanut and olive oil; maybe pastors should just use Crisco. Oh Pastor Hall, I think that your time is up. My home girls are looking at me crazy, and I'm looking at them crazy. Everybody is just crazy, including the members of the choir. Listening to some of them sing, I'd think that a few of them are possessed as well. Oh, I'm sorry, that wasn't lady like. I'm just ready to go. "Ma, can we leave now?" I nudged her lightly in the ribs. I know the answer to that question, wanting more to get on her nerves. She whipped her head around like she was about to karate chop me. She responded with the best church voice she could. You know the voice when everybody in the church professes to be so blessed-- you'd think that they fed thousands with a simple two fish and three loaves of bread. I'm just saying, church voice saints be the saints that be fronting on how they really feel. I don't have time for no religious rhetoric. I love Jesus, but I strongly dislike fake religious folk. And believe me, my mother knows how to fake it like a prostitute doing a quickie for twenty bucks.   "Of course we can't leave Precious. The pastor is still doing his thing. Why do you children have to grow up so fast? I remember when you just sat down like a little angel. No complaints, just sitting in perfect peace."

"That's because I was asleep mom, and I'm not little Precious anymore."

"You two be quiet." My father scolded us like we were both five year old girls. My mother and I must have forgotten that we were in church, but who can really forget with hard benches, air hotter in here than outside, and people spitting up their breakfast and dinner from last night. Yep, we are still at church. But my loving and sometimes mean father had to correct my mother and me, as she and I were having it out for each other as usual.

He went back to worship mode as he reached for his black leather bound Bible, slightly worn and torn from massive usage. You could barely see the pages of Songs of Solomon. That seems to be his favorite book of the Bible. Whoever says that the Bible doesn't speak of breasts and the love of a man and woman, then that person is a liar from the pits of hell. I'll personally cast out their demons for free ninety nine. As a matter of fact, in my opinion, the Bible has some of the greatest love stories ever written. All throughout the Bible it talks about the Love of God and how He loves his church and his people. We are his people, however corrupt we are; He still loves us. He just hates the sins we produce.

After my father's assault on our intelligence and mom's womanhood, she leaned over and gave him that oh no he didn't tell her to be quiet. But yes he did indeed. I am so happy, those two got back together. It seems like it's been the happiest time of their lives.

Approximately three years ago, we moved to Orlando to live there permanently. We visit Tallahassee on occasion, oftentimes to see family and old friends. Upon leaving the church we will be heading over to auntie's house, and then we are headed back to Orlando. Hopefully they have some chicken greased up at my aunt's house, because I am so hungry.

I really miss my brother, Justin; he always seemed like the great equalizer. My brother found the Lord and found some heathen women, up there in Atlanta. He promised to give me a tour of the city, come spring. Well, that hasn't happened yet. I'm not worried, though. I'm Atlanta bound one day, and that one day can't come soon enough.

"Say it with me church; deliver me Lord of my sins, so I shall not sin again. Wash the transgressions off my heart so that the sin in me shall depart. Cleanse me Lord God of the sins I say, in this Lord God, in this I pray. Cast out all demonic and earthly possessions." You can say that again.

Pastor Hall continued. "Make me right and ripe for the blessings. I but a man was born in sin. Lord God, oh Jesus, please take me back in. Neither am I a saint, but, yet a sheep laid down. Please Lord God, give me another crown. Fill me up with your morning dew so that I too can say I love you. No conviction lay down upon my mind, for Jesus died so I shall not hide."

How long is this going to last? Sounds like Pastor Hall must have run out of material. He's usually not the Shakespeare type. There he goes smiling wide again with those two gold front teeth.

"Ha-ha."

"Precious." My mother nudged me in the ribs; I didn't realize that I laughed in the middle of Pastor Halls' script, poem, or whatever you want to call it. Pastor Hall kept going on and on, putting a bold with italics b in boring.

"No guilt or shame shall cover me, for you oh God are my recipe. Do it for me like you did for the saints. And the congregation says, yes Lord Jesus, yes Lord Jesus we give you thanks! You are now dismissed." He bowed his sweat drenched head in humility. Sweaty palms and all couldn't stop him from delivering the word of God.

It sounds like the pastor was giving the poetic side

of deliverance. Deliverance is all that the pastor back in Orlando talks about.

All a young gal wants to know is how much deliverance is too much deliverance. Well, what do I know? I'm just a seventeen year old girl who's madly in love with herself. So maybe I need to be delivered from me. However that would work. That's not cute at all. Speaking of cute, my nails are due for a manicure. Since beauty is the definition of me, I have to make sure me is all that I'm supposed to be.

"Hey auntie, how are you?" I frowned, hungry as ever. I could eat a pig whole right about now; snout, tail, feet and all. Well maybe just a little baby piglet.   "Girl, I thought Pastor Hall locked the doors on you all, we've been over here ready to eat." She grinned, leaning over to take out the hot, made from scratch flaky biscuits, along with a cake size pan of Jiffy Cornbread. Her wide hips are very familiar to the kitchen as well. I believe she said that she puts on the most pounds with her sweet potato casserole, that's when her hips are really unforgiving. "Girl, you know how Pastor Hall is holding up services. He doesn't care how long it takes." My mother put her two cents in, makeup was smeared all over my mother 's face, as the humidity in that church could have put the clown business out of service just that day. I promise you, I did not see one lady walk out of First Baptist who didn't look like the Joker from Batman. "Well, the next time he decides to get long winded, you ought to shove a clock in his face and a piece of chicken on the pew; that will get his attention. I swear, as soon as he starts huffing and puffing scriptures, call the chicken place, they will be glad to come to the church. " Auntie said adamantly, fixing her eyes on my father in the process. I guess she wanted to get a good view of his reaction. "Ha---ha----ha," Everyone laughed in chorus. Auntie knows how to stir up trouble and make us laugh in the process. Well, she's not really my auntie; she's like my mom's best friend. I just call her auntie, and she loves it. She has two grown kids of her own. One is out in California trying to do the Hollywood thing, and the other is up in Alaska, doing the wilderness thing. Her husband passed away two years ago with brain cancer, her mother and father have been dead and gone. So we are kind of like the only family she got. She has a few brothers and sisters that stay up in Valdosta Georgia. Half the time they are on bad terms, which surprises me that they are here today to eat with us.

"Can someone please say the grace, preferably Deacon Rodney Lewis?" Auntie volunteered him.

"Yes I would," my dad said with a smile.

"Be short now Deacon, don't need the food getting colder than it already is," Auntie reprimanded.

"Just shove a clock and some chicken in his face like you told me." My mother blurted out at the table. The room roared once more, a spec of sweat danced off of my father's forehead, as the pressure for a quick and simple prayer clearly struck a nerve. Now if you know anything about my father, there is nothing quick and simple about Mr. Rodney Lewis. The man gets dressed longer than a woman. His prayers are no less than spiritual, and his conversations are generally filled with preachy undertones. But I love him though, there is something unique about how he makes me feel so special.   "Dear Gracious Father." You can tell this grace is about to be long. Any time someone starts with Dear Gracious Father, you know it's going to be a while before we eat.

"We thank you for this food and fellowship in the name of Jesus, we thank you for the carefully fried chicken, macaroni and cheese. We thank for the collards Lord God, the collards Lord Jesus, we praise you for the cornmeal that was put in place to raise the cornbread and the precious time it took to mix the Kool- Aid with water and sugar. And Lord we can't forget how blessed we are to have the candy yams on our table and a duck roasting in the oven. So with this Father we thank you for this food, this meal we pray. Amen, Amen, Amen.   "Boy I ought to slap you," Auntie winked at him and gave him the stupid look.   "You said to be short," He replied with a childish grin, wiping the sweat that transpired a few seconds ago. Ahh... The pressure is off of him, now we can finally eat. Where's my piglet?

"You're right, you can't trust a deacon or pastor to bless the meal, cause they'd bless the hell out of the food. And then go down the grocery list of things. Alright everyone I'm glad you all came, come on let's eat." Auntie was so excited to be amongst family and friends; she didn't know what to do with herself.

"Now that's what I'm talking about, I am so parched. Could you please hand me the Kool Aid?" I asked my dad, he looked at me with an unwilling gesture, but like the great father he is, he handed me the grape flavored sugar rich Kool-Aid. "You know Precious, you have really grown up. I ought to buy you a car this winter." He dug into his Mac n Cheese e while telling me this, mouth full of yellow.   "Really, really daddy, I knew you were the best," the little Precious came out of me. What was I thinking?

"Sike, that was a joke, don't have time for those teenage boys to be drooling all over you in the backseat." Now why does he have to be playing around like that.

I got all my feelings up and ready for that car, now he crushed me quickly. I don't even care if it was a beater, something better than nothing, although he knows better than to get me a beater. I ought to shove that duck down his throat and say sike.

"Daddy, why did you have to trick me in front of all these people?" His eyes were camouflaged between the duck, can't tell whether he was trying to duck my question, or he was just that hungry. I mean the food was good and all, but I lost my appetite. I guess I wasn't as hungry as I thought, or maybe it's because my father had hurt my feelings.

"I'm sorry Precious, I love you baby. Why did you have to grow up so fast? Why?" My daddy somberly glanced over at me. I hope he doesn't break down crying. I'll be leaving for college in a year, not the funeral home. Hopefully. "Ask God." I said contently, trying to find one of the most spiritual phrases I can think of to end the tension.

"Yeah, he already told me why." My daddy dropped his head.   "And what's that?"   My mother whispered, picking her head up from the yams she was stuffing in her mouth. With everyone around the table suddenly taking an interest in our conversation, I have suddenly found myself in the spotlight.   "We have to let go Sandra, and let God have control. We've raised her right, and we should be proud to have a daughter who has chosen to be pure and holy be-

17

fore the Lord. But after she reaches eighteen and hits the cracks of our doors, my Little Precious is no longer under our command. She is a part of the body of Christ, and we pray that God keeps her, sustains her, and continues to lead her in the way which she should go."

My mother's tears slide down her face like a roller coaster waiting for gravity to pull it down. I guess my father has always been the poetic one.

"I'm proud of you baby, but I know I must let you go. It's been a long ride and an even longer journey, but what can I say." My daddy blushed as he told me this. He's so handsome, gouging down the last bit of crumbs on his plate. He's not the only one to finish their meal, while my plate looks barely touched. With stomachs protruding further than usual and belching sounds arriving every second, I can only imagine the bathroom will be doing overtime on a Sunday. For Heaven's sake, even the toilet can't get a day of rest.

"I love you daddy." I'm such a sucker for him. He is definitely my first love.   "I love you too, Precious." I hope my mother doesn't feel bad, this is kind of like one of those father-daughter moments.

"Break it up; this is not a going away party. My God, the girl is only in the eleventh grade, Rodney. Senior year hasn't come yet. Besides, I hate to see folks crying over chickens and ducks," my Auntie stated, with her country humor.

"Hey, my daughter is about to graduate next year, we must begin to plan now for her future." He playfully raised his voice; auntie wasn't content with his comments.   "Deacon you should have been planning for the girl's future before she was born!" Her tone changed from casual playful to mildly serious, no one at the table was expecting that sort of response. The members of the table morphed to ultra quiet. Even a feather dropping to the ground would have been too loud for the stillness and question marks written over everyone's face in the dining room. "I'm talking about graduation parties and stuff. Why do you always have to trip on me?" My dad took offense.

"Because you are easy to trip on honey, that's why. You know I love you Rodney. Might have hated your guts, the ten years ago when you and Sandra were split up. But now you finally decided to be a man. Look at you wearing the pants in the family. How's ya lil boy doing, you know, the one that you had fornicating with that hamburger lady."

"Alright, alright, that's enough. What's gotten into you, sister girl? My Rodney is a changed man. No need to throw up the past on the brother."   My mother gave Auntie the cold shoulder; Auntie reeked with such disbelief, till she left a wet spot on her right cheek. That's right; though, what mama said. My dad has changed a lot, and they are doing exceptionally well. If it wasn't for my dad being around, showing me what real love looks like, I think I would've lost my virginity two years ago.

There was this handsome regular guy. I was so lusting over him, when I first got into high school. I was a freshman, at the time. He was a junior. He wasn't the athletic type or a musician; he just knew how to make a girl laugh and feel comfortable around him.

He was the melt in your mouth not in your hands type of brotha, with hot chocolate skin, you know the creamy type without any blemishes and oh a gift for gab, he put my lustful creativity into overdrive and I'm surely not talking about PG13 type of stuff. He definitely was the talk of the school, if he wasn't, I don't know who was? The brotha had a gift for gab and he was an obvious magnet for women, opposites do attract you know, and I was attracted to Kenneth Green.

To make a long story short, the brother and I ended up talking a little. He told me some things about his life, his past relationships, and he talked about God. I just thought that he was the perfect gentleman. Oh, and did I mention that he was cute? So week after week, he and I were getting closer and closer. So close, till I got a detention for skipping class. Of course my mother found out about it, immediately, because she works at the same school I attend. That was not good. After coming up with some lies to tell my mom about why I skipped class, she came up with the conclusion that it was a guy. Yep, I couldn't hide anything from my mother. She immediately told me to stay away from Kenneth Green, I thought she was tripping. All that did was draw me closer and closer to him. He pulled out all his player cards on me when he found out my mother didn't want us together. As if my mother's schooling wasn't enough, my dad sat me down and had a real deep conversation with me, kind of like the one today. Being the preacher man deacon he is, he said one thing I will never forget, "If the guy asks you to have sex but does not offer you a ring, lose him; for he is but a wolf in sheep's clothing."   I nodded my head to show some signs that I agree, really to blow him off and finish the sermon. With Kenneth spitting his sermons to me, and daddy preachy, I didn't know which message to believe. Of course my teenage feelings were craving the words Kenneth was spitting, but on the flip side, I knew that what my daddy said was more than right. It's God's way. Huh, the struggle of being a teenager in a family of Christians, at least if I was a heathen child I didn't have to worry about the guilt of taking it to third base with Kenneth. And believe me; the brotha was more than ready to satisfy every creative thought I ever had of him. A month after talking with my dad Kenneth popped the question. Oh my I said to myself, this brotha is about to give me a ring. But wait, I am too young to marry. What's the legal age to marry in Florida? I knew mommy and daddy were wrong about this guy; he sincerely wants to be with me. We will live and love forever, have chocolate chip babies and be high school sweethearts. And now I can get my groove on legally. We will buy us a house with the money we don't have and it will be in a gated community with the white picket fence and the no car garage. The wedding will be extravagant; it will be different, but extravagant. The theme will be white and red, the white will signify my purity before God and the red will signify the blood of Jesus over our marriage. Wow. Is this really what love feels like? Unfortunately my fantasy wedding was interrupted by, "are you ok, Kenneth asked. And at that moment I was brought back to reality of what he really asked me, the boy asked me to have sex with him. He knew that I was a virgin, so he gave me the trademark line, "I'm going to make sure it doesn't hurt you." He looked down at his feet, embarrassed by what he suggested, but in a cute kind of way.   With my emotions pent up, my dad on my mind, and God obviously near my side, I asked Kenneth one simple question, 'do you have a ring for me?' He paused for about ten seconds playing in his pockets, and then looking back at me dumbfounded, of course he doesn't have a ring, what was I thinking to ask that. Silly me, he's too young to get married. So then I told him, 'Oh, I'm too young to have sex.'

And then I left him like that, cold turkey. I guess he was a wolf in sheep's clothing. A funny, cute and special wolf though. I miss him. Kenneth was a cool guy and all, but my daddy has taught me too much about love and love will find a way to get me a ring if it wants to do anything. Lord keep me. I surely don't want to end up like Ms. Hamburger, going from man to man to man. I want one man and one man only, and he better love me like my daddy. Yep, I'm a daddy's girl, always been, always will be.

"Girlfriend, I love me a man that can cook," Auntie's sister Genie said. "Why love you a man that can cook, when you can cook your man." My mom devilishly said, licking her lips and batting her eyes at daddy. That is so nasty; they need to leave that kind of marital stuff for the bedroom. I don't want to hear that, or see their little calls from the wild. "Hey Sandra, today is Sunday. Ain't no time to talk about no freaky stuff on Sunday. Save that conversation for tomorrow. Today is the Lord's Day, and this is the day that the Lord has made. We shall rejoice, and be glad in it." Genie said, yelling all over the place as if Sunday is the only day to be holy. Quietness ensued once more; all eyes are on ma and dad now.

"Every day is the Lord's Day; he built us, and he built this earth. We ought to be holy and righteous, no matter the day, the time, or the place. God knows all, sees all, and searches the hearts of men constantly." That's my daddy, preaching the word like he never preached it before. He should be a preacher. My daddy can quote scriptures faster than a math teacher quoting algebra.   "Said like a true champ," my mother said with cheeks wider than a hot biscuit covered in gravy with hot sauce on the top.   Ding-ding-ding let the fight begin. On the left side is my father weighing about two twenty-five, standing at about six feet lean build. On the right side is always in somebody's business Genie standing at a mere five feet six inches and also weighing two twenty-five. Let's get ready to rumble!!!

"What do you know about God, Deacon?" Uh oh, Genie is drunk. Passing the keys to the car, sounds like a good idea.

"I know that God has restored my life, my wife, and my family. So practically, I could stop right there. But, I won't," His face stiffened up a bit, "because God is much better than that. You asked who God is, so I'm going to tell you who he is to me.   When I wake up in the morning, the air from his spirit fills my lungs up all the way to the top till I can't inhale any more. At that very moment, I know that's God. When the engine in my body, which is my heart, transfers the blood from my heart down to my legs I know that's God." Oh he's preaching now, and we the congregation are clinging on to his every word.

"When the blood continuously keeps pumping so that I can balance myself, I know that's God.

When my stomach secretly tells my brain that it's hungry, I know that's God. When I get a sudden ache because I bruised my knee on the bathroom cabinet, I know that's God. When I go outside in one hundred degree temperatures and sweat pours all over my body, I know that's God.

For if I did not have the sweat, my body wouldn't have the ability to cool off, therefore saving me from the heat. I can go on and on about why I know God, but here's a hint. When you wake up tomorrow, count how many breaths you take, how many moves you make, and how many thoughts you think per second." He takes a breath for a moment as if to give Genie an example of what he just said. Judging by the lines in his face and sunken dimples, he's not happy.

Before Genie could react to my father's statements, he quickly interjected with a few more choice words. "It is God who blew the breath of life into Adam, and with that same breath, we breathe today. If God didn't breathe life into him, then Adam would just be a molten sculpture made of clay, which you would find in the museum today. But my God actually made an animated man, one who can walk, run, swim, create, and most importantly, love God with all his heart and lean not unto his own understanding."

"Amen, amen," Auntie interjected, trying to bring peace and a little laughter to a storm she knew was about to come. "Boy what they train ya'll on down there in Orlando? Got you prophesying round here like you died and rose in three days. I knew you were deep, but not that deep, Rodney. God bless you, sir. God bless you." Everyone went back to their normal conversation; my mother was over near my dad comforting him and using a clean white handkerchief to wipe the sweat from his eyebrows and all around the smaller, more intricate parts of his face. The wrinkles which were highly visible a moment ago have now disappeared and everything seemed to be back to normal. Until....The storm that Auntie predicted would come. Well it came alright, and with it was a mean and nasty vigor, maybe even a hatred embedded in her tone.

"He ain't nothing!" Genie said, drunker than two guys at a bar taking shots for an hour. I doubt she understood a word my daddy said to her. She did manage to get everyone's attention and make the room fall silent once more.

"Don't listen to her, Rodney; she's just an old drunk with a tude. That heffa' don't know when to shut her mouth at times," Auntie said with a look of displeasure written all over her face.

My daddy was looking at Genie like he was ready to lose his religion. My mother breaks the unnerving silence, "Well it is getting late. It's about time we head on back down to Orlando; we have school in the morning."

"Okay, darlings, you all be safe on the road," Auntie told us with a genuine love and caring for our well-being.

Just when keys were in hand and the three of us were a few inches from the door. Genie erupted again, just like a good drunk would, "Wait a minute, wait a minute ole' Deacon Rodney. Tell me this, son." Now she is being disrespectful, she called my grown father the name that old slave masters called the men on the field 'son and boy'. What is her deal? How disrespectful!

She opens her mouth again. Oh no, no telling what she's about to say next. "Tell me this now, Rodney. How could you honestly tell if somebody's demon possessed? I mean, I---, I---, just want to know." She slurred her words.   "Usually, when a person is acting like you're acting, we come to the conclusion that you are possessed." Wow, that was cold, and pretty funny at the same time. "Um, um say that again Deacon." Her eyes pierced forward like a rat scouring for cheese. Needless to say, she may find herself in a trap.

"I said, usually when a person, such as yourself, is acting the way you are acting this evening, we determine that you are demon possessed." He did not back down.   "Is that so? "Well I ought to--"   Before she could even finish, my dad says, "Yeah, you're possessed with the spirits of Bud and Weiser. I cast that out of you in the name of Jesus Christ!"   The roars of laughter filled the room once more, funny to see how all these grown adults are giggly like little kids.

"Hold me back; hold me back. I'm about to get unrighteous in this place. This Deacon is about to be baptized with my bat and sanctified with my right fist. I'm gone, send you to the Lord right now; you say another word about me." If there is anybody bound to the grave, it has to be her drunken butt, I'm sure her liver and kidneys are working over time just to sustain her.

"Time to go, Rodney; let's go. You know how Genie gets, when she gets drunk. Come on, Precious, pack your things and let's go." My mother tried to be reasonable about the whole situation, but I can look at my mother and tell she has some pent up feelings about the whole thing. Genie always cast a dark shadow on seemingly good moments with family and friends.

However the outcome, drama never stops. I'm so ready to go, anyway. Maybe we overstayed our welcome. Maybe Auntie's sister is possessed, and if so, they better make sure they find her a bucket.

DEPRESSED

There is nothing worst than the smell of cold fungus, thirty five different human odors, a windowless classroom with beige painted walls, and a teacher who looks like she woke up out of her rocking chair. Yes, this is my classroom; I'd like to call jail. The whole color scheme and not having windows has jail and depression written all over it. It's depressing enough to be in school.

With dingy and dirty classrooms like this and someone's great grandmother at the podium teaching us, it kind of ruins the fun in learning. I know that it's been like massive budget cuts and all over the state of Florida and our current governor has the brains of a five year old, at least that's what my father said. Either way, it doesn't matter how smart the governor is, I'm sure he should be smart enough to know that this ain't right. Students deserve to have a better environment for our education. And they call this school Morning Glory. The only glory I get from this place is the time the bell rings for me to go home. A girl like me loves to be cute. I love to be fly. I don't have time for no compromise. Hey, what else can I say? I'm a girl. This classroom is all so against my conservative nature; it's just a little too liberal for me. I need to complain to someone, somebody help me. Help me Jesus. Alright, looks like the teacher is finally ready to teach, if I was apart of the fashion police, I would fine her old butt two-hundred dollars for that aged polka dot dressed she got on. Not only does it make her look her age, but she looks like she belongs in a museum somewhere on display, not in front of a classroom full of teenagers with raging youthful feelings for each other. Lord God, if only I can get through this day, I promise I'll wash the dishes without mama telling me to.

"Class we are here to go over our algebraic expressions; would you please turn to page sixty-six? That's sixty-six students. Page sixty-six," Mrs. Applegate repeated. Why does she have to repeat herself three times, not like we are wearing hearing aids like her?

"Now can someone," her voice cracks, "tell me the meaning of pi?" Yeah, I can tell her the meaning of "pie." Auntie made us a good apple pie last night. I hope my daddy didn't eat the leftovers.

"No volunteers," she looked around the room, "Oh, I see a hand up now, let me fix my glasses to see who it is. Is that the young lady

Stacy?" She still squinched a bit, barely able to recognize any of us. I guess its first day of school jitters for us all. It's going to be a long semester. She should be embarrassed; that's James. How much does it take to get rid of an insignificant teacher like her?

"I'm James, Ma'am," he looked highly offended, gritting his teeth and complaining under his breath.

"I'm sorry darling; I must not have cleaned my glasses well enough. These glasses can sometimes be a bugga to an old lady like me. Continue on young man; tell us what the meaning of pi is."

James willfully obliged, "Pi is the sum equation of the numbers destined to fall in love with each other. Therefore, they create a circle of trust, known as pi." Look at him trying to sound all intelligent and sexy at the same time; he is still my favorite nerd. "Although I like your description, Mr. James I must say that you are wrong. But before we get to the real meaning of pie, and if you are talking about the pie you eat, you are wrong again. We will look into the meaning of pi shortly, but first I have a little bit more trivia for you, my precious students." She sounds a little devilish, if you ask me. Maybe this granny is really a witch, or maybe just maybe she forgot to take her meds.

On to her next victim, "Brandy, will you come up and show the class the multiplication property of one?" Mrs. Applegate is humped over the podium, her face seemed to have dropped a bit, and clear signs of tiredness have suddenly wreaked havoc on her composure.

"Who me?" Brandy asked nonchalantly, the girl acts like she wasn't called on.   "Yes, you, darling. I did not stutter." I guess a response from a ditsy girl like Brandy will wake anyone up. "Brandy to the board at once, young lady!" Her patience for ignorance has dwindled.   "But I don't know anything about a multiplication property of something." She yelled back at the teacher, pouting in the process. Her lips look like they can touch the tip of her chin. Oh Brandy.

"Property of one," the teacher looked at her with grave disapproval. "Would anyone else like to give it a shot?" Her heavy sense of frustration seemed to come in the form of her tapping her feet to the floor like the jazz players of old. Yet, the music to her ears are sweaty and sexually frustrated teenagers who could care two cents less about math. Unlike a jazz piece, the melody she hears from us cannot be soothing in anyway. Maybe   she   should   just   retire. Finally someone raised their hand, and with that acknowledgement Mrs. Applegate regained her strength, her composure, and the tapping of the feet ceased. An overly excited and enthusiastic James, took to answering the question "I know what the property of one is Mrs. Applegate." With his deep black tender eyes, boyish smile and cute swagger, you would have thought that Mrs. Applegate was waving five dollars in front of that boy. "Not you again, Mr. James. We've already had enough of your cookie cutter antics. Besides, give someone else a chance to speak. Is there anyone else willing and able to come right up to the board here?" She paused for a few seconds, searching our eyes, looking to see if anyone has the will or the heart to answer her question. " No volunteers, huh? Okay, Mr. James, you better be right. Back in my day, if you had a wrong answer, you would get the ruler to the buttocks. These days you kids are so protected, till you wouldn't get the ruler for committing murder." "What's wrong with you youth of the day?" Mrs. Applegate continues her rant. "You all are so dumb. You young girls strutting your stuff around from here to the North Pole and expect a young fellow to think that you are pure and righteous. That's furthest from the truth, young ladies. Did Mother Teresa wear the short shorts that you ladies are wearing? No, she was covered up as a lady should be."

Of course none of what she's talking about has anything to do with math. She's just a mean old hag who loves to go on her rants from time to time. I guess she doesn't have anyone to talk to back at the house, because she always seems to take it out on us. "Class, what was I talking about?" The teacher looked around with frustration. She lost her bearings and probably a few screws in the head too. "You were talking about James going up to the board, until you went on one of your rants," one of my classmates schooled her. Walking towards the front, James picks up the black marker next to the teachers desk, opens up his mouth, and says, "The multiplication property of one is something like this. If "a" is a real number then 'a x 1 = 1 x a = a.' Hey did I get it right, teacher lady?"

"Don't teacher lady me, boy! Call me Grandma; all my students call me Grandma, got that?" Her glasses slowly dipped below her nose. "Yes, ma'am." James jumped back, and then walked away from the board to his seat. "By the way, son, good job. You had me squinting a little with your small handwriting, but I can see. I can see it now. Class let's do another problem. Are there any volunteers? Alright, that's it; I'll start picking people out. Sonya, I need you to come to the board for me, darling. You've been quiet for too long." "I don't feel so good," Sonya whispered to the teacher. "Well I beg to differ," the teacher announced. "I said I don't feel so good. My tummy aches, and I'm not good in math. Can I take a pass?" She balled up, wanting to escape from an awkward moment. Who is this girl? "Little one, little one, here me out. The only pass you get in life is a sign that says R.I.P. on your tombstone. I'm a little old lady, and I have never received a pass." That's because you're not dead yet. She makes no sense what-so-ever. If she's going to come up with these half hearted analogies, she better make sense of them. "So get your little rump up here, now, young lady!" Wow, where did that come from? Now, she has the girl crying. Let me rescue this girl before it gets out of control.   "I'll come up to the board", I raised my hand for attention.   "Well if it isn't little Mss. Precious, thinks she 'all that,' because her mommy teaches here. I'm not going to be light on you either, little girl." Calm down Precious you can handle this, calm down. I said back and forth in my mind.

"What question do you have for me, teacher lady?" I gave her the third degree.
It's Grandma!" She raised her voice at me. "Okay, Grandma, what's your question?" She's about to make me explode. "Come up to the board, and show the class the meaning of the associate property of addition. And just because you attend 'Morning Glory High School,' doesn't mean you need to have an attitude with me. Didn't your mother teach you how to speak to your elders?" She has a lot of nerve. It's okay, I'm cool. I'm just going to call on the name of, Jesus, Jesus, Jesus, to keep me from going black on her butt.

"You can come to the board sometime, Lady Precious." Oooh I hate her guts.   As I got up, I looked over to the right and still saw Sonya wet with tears. Crying, looking depressed, sad, and lonely. I wish I could help her, right now, but I've already done my best by practically being humiliated myself. I love people, but I can't do everything. I'm only one person. The girl, Sonya, needs to get a hall pass, report to the restroom, and wipe these tears from her eyes.   "The associate property of addition goes a little something like this. If a, b, and c are real numbers, then '(a + b) +c = a+ (b + c).' There is definitely nothing hard about this class. If you don't understand this, then you probably wouldn't get anything loosely related to Algebra. By the way, Grandma, that was wrong the way you treated Sonya. As a matter of opinion, it was also very wrong the way you treated me, too. For an old lady your age, you should have a little more dignity about yourself." Yes I said it, and the whole class roared with laughter, you would have thought   I   was   doing   stand   up. "Get out my class, young lady; get out my class at once." She pointed at the door while waiving a pink   detention   slip. "Okay, oh, you don't have to be a witch about it. I'll get my stuff and leave. I'm happy anyways." If there was anything my daddy taught me, he taught me to treat people the way they want to be treated. I couldn't stand there and watch Sonya cry with the teacher smiling with pleasure.

Exiting the room, Sonya slipped a yellow note for me to read. The girl was still shedding puppy tears, "thank you for what you did for me. Can we talk later?" She said, under the auspice of a swollen throat and what looks to be a swollen heart. This is not cool; something else has to be wrong with this girl beyond what the teacher has done. "Sure, meet me in the ladies room in about an hour."   "Okay, thanks." She barely   picked   her   head   up. Walking down the hall way, towards my mother's class, I opened up the note written on bright yellow legal pad type of paper, and it read…. Thanks for standing up for me, I hope that maybe we could be friends now. The girl had to give me this big piece of paper to tell me this; she has weird written all over her. But I don't mind being the girl friend; she looks like she could use a friend. What would Jesus do? And what in the world am I thinking, I can't go to my mother's class right now, she'll slap me from here to Easter if she found out I got kicked out of class. Maybe I should just chill for a minute. I need to find a spot where I can't get caught. No need to get in any more trouble.

"Precious, are you in here? Precious can you here me?"   "Yeah girl, I'm in here, just handling my business right quick, why you whispering girl. I'll be with you in a few seconds." Lord help her.   Please   Lord,   help   me   too.

After flushing the toilet, I see a desperate Sonya waiting for me at the sink, looks like she has the whole legal pad in her hand now. "Hey Precious, um--um-- I kind of like communicate better when I write things to people. So forgive me but what I have to tell you is in this note. I hope you understand, but I got to go." She hurried to the door. "But wait, I don't even know what's your favorite color?" I pleaded. "I don't have a favorite, but if I did, it would be gray." She grasped the door handle, opening it just enough to move her small frame through, she has to be no more than one-hundred and five pounds at about five feet seven inches. Just before she slipped away, I tried to pry another question from her. "But what about boys, you have a boyfriend?" "No, and bye Precious, I'll see you around. Don't lose that note there," and just like that she vanished with the drones of other students roaming the hallway at the ring of the bell. I hope she didn't waste my time for another fairy tell note. Does this girl have a thing for me? Ugh... I hope that's not what this is about.

I carefully and meticulously opened up the mystery letter this time. I don't understand why she just couldn't talk to me about this face to face. No one ever stood up for me like that, I feel like you are like my new hero. My father is a drunk and a major abuser. He always hits on me and my mom. Sometimes my mother has a black eye for a week, and she ends up taking off work because he tells her so. She's so afraid of him and no one speaks up for her. One night my father came in about eleven o'clock and he just went off on all four of us; me, my mom and my two younger brothers. I started talking back and he hit me so hard that I not only lost one of my teeth, but I fell back five feet on to the kitchen table and bruised my rib in the process. My mother just stood there watching and not saying a word. My two younger brothers are too young to do anything. I hate my life, I hate my dad, and I even hate God for allowing this to continue to happen to me. I am so helpless. Thought about running away, but I feel he would only get worse with my mom and two brothers if I did. He told me that if I called the police, or any one for that matter, he said he will kill us all. I am so scared, I feel so down, so lonely and don't know what to do. Thanks for being that light for me today. I'm tired of being used and abused by people. I hope one day we could be friends. Please don't tell anybody about this. I just don't know what to do, and I kind of felt like you was someone I could probably trust. My knees buckled and tears poured down my eyes like the Niagara Falls, if anyone saw me, they would have thought that I was apart of the attraction. It's not funny; my tears could not be controlled. She had one more part to that note that disturbed my heart. I don't want us to die like some of the people I see on T.V. Why are we abused? What did we ever do to deserve this? Why can't my mom stand up to him? Do you think I should kill him?

TRANSGRESSED

Well, I didn't actually go to my mother's classroom. After reading that letter, I broke down crying like a tormented baby for at least a good thirty minutes. I was shaking in the stall, feeling the pressures of her pain put onto my soul. I didn't want to leave the bathroom. I just wanted to tear up and worship the Lord. Giving him thanks that I'm not going through that mess. Yeah Daddy cheated on Mom and all, but it could have always been worse. I cried, and I cried, and I cried, all the way till the bell rang for us to switch classes again. I was drained. My Physical Education class followed so I had a little more time to bury myself in grief as we stretched out.

"How was your day in school, Precious? You seem a little sad." My mother announced, as if she could see right through my spirit. "I'm okay, Mother. I'm just tired from a long day in school. I'm a little hungry. Are you cooking dinner tonight?"   "Well, of course I am. I'll be cooking ribs and baked beans; your favorite dish. What do you think about that?" I could puke at the thought of food.

All I want to consume right now is a good few minutes of sleep. I could see now that I could never make the cut to be a school counselor. "Thanks." I said unexcitedly, knowing it is my favorite. It's just not the right time. Feels like Sonya threw me an eighty mile per hour pitch with no glove on to catch what she threw at me. "You don't sound so happy, but I'm not going to push it on you. When you're ready to talk just let me know, and we'll talk. Dinner should be ready in about two hours. Get some rest, baby, get some rest." As much as I would love the proposition to sleep, the last thing I can think about doing is getting rest. Here I have a classmate thinking about killing her father, and I'm not supposed to tell anyone about it. "Lord, you know about her problems better than I do. I pray that you do something with that family, before it's too late.

"Precious, dinner is ready baby. Dinner is ready, baby girl, wake up. Your father will be here in ten minutes; don't want him waiting on you for supper. Precious can you hear me girl?" I can hear her, but my good sleep wants to do nothing more than ignore her for the rest of the night. Forget family dinner. "Yes, yes, I hear you. I just, just was in a deep sleep." "Well, snap out of it, and wash up. You have eight minutes, now, before he arrives." "He who?" I asked her, looking around entering the kitchen sleepy and confused. "Your father, silly, you didn't drink anything unusual before you went to sleep, did you?" "Mother," I looked at her like she was crazy. Is that what she thinks about me sometimes? "Alright, alright, calm your little nerves," She politely scolded me. It was cute, but totally uncalled for.   I am so exhausted; I really don't know what to do. It seems like I fell twenty floors down an elevator. I feel so dizzy. Why does dinner have to be ready now? Why can't it just be ready in the morning? I hear a key opening up the door. It's Daddy. "Daddy, Daddy," The little Precious came out of me once more. Hey, what can I say, I'm a daddy's girl.   My daddy walked in the front door with a big wide grin on his face and open arms ready to receive me. "Hey Precious, give me a hug my love. Hello Sandra, how are you?" "Well, I'm glad somebody was able to motivate her. She wouldn't get up for the president. Are you feeling better now Precious?" She scanned my face, looking for anything that would say other wise. I tried hard to feel better, but a mother's intuition will always scoop out the cover ups. "A little", I lied, besides daddy's presence, I didnt feel much better. This Sonya situation has really got me torn. I hope that she's worth all the agony and frustration she's putting me through. That child needs Jesus.   "What's wrong, sweet heart? Is someone bothering you at school?" It's not a matter of someone bothering me, but something is bothering me. My dad cares and loves me so much, that he will go out to that school and put whoever wants to mess with me in their misery. My daddy is strong, powerful, and very protective of me. He won't let me or mother get hurt, at least not if he has the chance to stop it. My daddy doesn't play. He always told me that the job of a Lewis man is to protect the family and feed the flock. This is what he's been trying to groom Justin to do. Of course Justin is a fool and continues to reject our daddy's advice. Oh well. I guess he'll learn one day.

Sort of reminds me of my father God in heaven; always watching, always loving, always protecting me. He makes sure no one tries to hurt me, unless it's his will for that situation to happen. I'm so happy that God loves me; it makes me feel like I was born in Heaven as I go through all this Hell. "Sweetie, if there is anything, anything whatsoever that you would like to talk about, I promise you can come to me or your mother, and we can work it out." "I'm okay." In reality, I was lying to him, but held to secrecy with my new friend. My mother couldn't wait anymore for the small talk, she was ready to eat. "Well, let's eat!" My mother said the prayer as we all held hands, thanking God for blessing us with a good meal to eat. "How was work today, baby?" my mother looked over to my father.   "It was alright, got a little stressed out. A couple of people I had to let go because the boss said we need to bring in more Mexicans to save him on cost. I don't know how much longer I can do this construction job. I don't even know when they'll up and replace me, but I'm just tired of having to fire good, hardworking, respectable people to save the boss on cost. I mean, we are making millions, for him, and that's still not enough. I have nothing against the Mexicans, but I find myself firing more of my own and hiring more of them. There should at least be a balance. Forget the stereotypes, the few blacks and whites I have left on the job site do work hard and pull their own weight. But unfortunately I may be forced to fire them as well."   His once glowing smile that he walked through the door with has now curved to a dismal frown, the true colors of how his day went. Stress and frustration maligned through out his face, dispelling the true nature of his beautiful white teeth and boyish smile.   Daddy could have been a model back in the day; he's one of the most handsome men I know. Maybe Justin will eventually inherit daddy's good looks and good nature.

Of course mama tries to save the day," Its okay, baby, the world doesn't always work the way we may like it to work. But don't blame it on the Mexicans. Blame it on the greedy boss. Look at our next door neighbor Felipe; he's hardly ever home. He's steady out there on the farm working to feed five mouths at the house. Don't you think he deserves to have a good paying job with benefits, too? It's only you, me, and Precious living at the house, and even we sometimes struggle to make ends meet. I applaud Felipe's efforts, and I also applaud you too." Mama always knows how to look at things with a third eye, which makes so much sense. The Mexican people are people just like us, they need essential food, and clothing, and they are God's children too.   "I know baby; I'm just mad the way things are going down. I have to do all the dirty work. I've been thinking about going back in to business for myself. I don't have to deal with the pain of firing my own by being my own boss."   He comforted himself with a rib and baked beans; I hate to see my daddy feeling so sad. He does deserve better, he was doing real good with his website development business at one point, I don't know why he closed it   down. "But what about Felipe's pain, honey? He's out there sweating bottles of water to make a living for his family. And if you ask me, they seem to be pretty   good   people." "I have no problem with Felipe, darling. I just have a   problem   with   the   system,   honey." It's time to change the subject on these two fools. God knows I would love nothing more than to talk about something else. This conversation is just too depressing.

"So, you two don't mind me dating a cute Mexican boy? I think I'll like a guy that will make me say 'hola.'"   "Don't you start any mess up in here, Precious. Your father doesn't want you dating anyone," my mother gasped, as she tried to catch the little breath she had left after my comment. My daddy was surprisingly unmoved by what I said. "I wouldn't say that I don't want Precious dating. I just want to know the dude she's dating. Like I said the other day, we've done our best, and God will be with her as she embarks on the road to college." I love my father, he could be tough, but he's also a man of reason. I can appreciate that. "I would rather her not date and focus on her schooling,"   my   mother   said   stiffly. "We will talk about this after dinner, baby. You know, maybe between the late night show and gospel," he tries to iron out the wrinkles in the conversation.

Late night show! Please, I know that's code word for marital relations, don't really know what he was referring to when he mentioned gospel, but, ok.   I'll   be   the   fool   this   time. "Okay, Rodney, I'm cool with that. So, Precious, what's been bothering you?   And who do you like?" Oh no, she had to go back to that. I thought she wasn't bringing this subject back up. I really don't want to think about Sonya right now. And as for boys, I don't have time for them.

"Mother, I'm fine, I guess I just needed some rest at the time, and I don't like any boys. Boys are like yesterday."   "What do you mean by that?" my mother asked me with a wide grin on her face. You would of thought she won a championship game with that smile, I guess that's the pleasure she gets when she hears that I'm not that interested in guys at this moment, especially after the last fellow just tried to get the password   to   my   panties. "I just don't have time for boys. It's not like they aren't cute and all, but I'm just satisfied with being a loner for now."   "Okay, well, your father and I will have a little conversation about that tonight. In the meantime, you are dismissed to do your homework. Don't stay on the phone and internet all night either." "Okay." Sometimes my mother still wants to treat me like a little kid. I'm not saying that I'm grown and have my own home. I'm just saying, I'm tired of being treated, like I said before, like Little Precious. Maybe I should call my brother, and see how he's doing. Maybe I should call my home girl Maxine. She has the dirt on everything happening around the school. I can use the juiciness right about now; need to let off a little steam. Maxine is so funny. She could have me laughing all night. I guess I'll call my brother first. He is such a sad situation sometimes.

        "Hey, Justin, how you doing up there in Atlanta?" I listened to him release a whirlwind of air through my receiver. What is he doing? "Trying to catch my breath; so many good looking honeys up here, I need to repent." Laugh out loud, my brother is insane. "Justin, that's all you talk about; girls and more girls. How are you doing in school?" "I'm cool with school." He said nonchalantly, there must be something wrong. "What ever happened with you and Alicia?" Alicia was his main squeeze for a while when we were living in Tallahassee, I believe their relationship kind of fell of a bit ever since we moved to Orlando and he moved to Atlanta for school. "We still talk." He said that like he didn't want to hear a word I had to say about Alicia. Oops, my bad for bringing up a sore subject. "Ya'll still talk about what?" I love to press the issues. I'm sure he's probably fuming at the mouth now. "We talk about life. Come on, Precious, why you trying to be all up in my business? I don't have any dirt to tell you, like your friend Maxine." "I just care about you, and I know that God has a better plan for you than just being a womanizer." "I'm cool with God; he understands that he gave me hormones too. I can't help it that I love many different women." "But do you love God the same way?" Maybe I took this question a little too far. "Yeah, well not like I should," he said with a pause. "You're right; I need to do better by God. He's brought me this far. The temptation up here is just outrageous, Precious. You'll see next year when you go to college." "Yeah, but I'm staying a virgin." At least I hope I could. "You do that, Precious, you do that. You got something that I'll never be able to get back." He said that without any conviction. "Justin, can I ask you a question?" "Go ahead." He sounds a little irritated with me now. "Why do boys only care about sex?" This is an excellent question in my book.

"It's not that we only care about sex, it's just based on the fact that it feels so good. For example, what is it that you love to do best?" "I love to go to the movies with my girlfriends." "Why?" He started breathing heavy again. "Because it's fun, Justin!" What's his point? "Exactly, sex is a whole lot of fun. You wouldn't keep going to the movies if you weren't having fun, right, Precious." "Alright, but going to the movies is not a sin. Sex outside of marriage is. You see, just as well as going to the movies is not a sin based on the content of that movie. So sex is not a sin based on the context of marriage?" Wow, I'm starting to sound like my step brother Joseph and Pastor Hall. "Why you always got to preach to me? I know what sin is and what's not; it's just so hard for me to stop. That's why I don't like answering your questions; you always seem to make me look like the worst heathen in the world." "I'm sorry, big brother. Sometimes I just get scared when thinking about sex. Everyone in high school is practically doing it. And many times I feel alone because I'm not." "Precious, Precious, don't feel that way. Look, there is going to be some guy that comes around and falls in love with you, and who knows, he may just be a virgin too. I know that you can't use me as the best example when it comes to relationships, but I guess I can be an example of what to avoid when dating."

You got that right. "So what's really going on with you and Alicia?" I just got to know; maybe I'm becoming more like the queen of getting dirt Maxine.

"You are a nosey little girl. We, we just haven't been on speaking terms like we used to be. I think she knows all about my wild behaviors since being up here in ATL. I really don't know what's next for her and I. Right now, we are just friends." "Okay." I guess his lame answer was good enough for me. "Well, I have this honey who supposed to be coming through tonight, so I'm going to let you go, lil sis. I love you, keep your head up and stay pure, good night." "Good night." My brother does not do right by women; telling me to keep my head up and stay pure while he got some girl coming by his place. Justin ought to be ashamed of himself. Lord, I pray that Justin doesn't catch any S.T.D's or get any girls pregnant. This I pray in Jesus name, amen.

"Girl what have you been hearing around Morning Glory High School these days?" I curiously tried to get the dirt from my friend Maxine. She couldn't hold water if she was given a well to hold it in. "I heard that you're friends with that Sonya chick. Sister girl, leave that whore alone. News has it the girl got too much baggage. Some say the chick is about to go psycho in a few days. I'm talking some Columbine stuff. I'm talking some stuff that will send you to Hell if you ain't right; to Heaven if you believe in Jesus Christ." She was pretty adamant. "No, no, the girl is not like that Maxine. Give her a chance to prove herself." In the back of my mind, I've just became afraid of Sonya. Maxine may be a big mouth, but ninety percent of the stuff she says is either happening or ends up happening. Let's hope what she's saying about Sonya is apart of the ten percent of information that ends up wrong. "She done brainwashed you too, Precious? Wow, she's good. I heard the chick got a lot of stuff going down with her mother and father." Maxine said judgingly.

"We need to help her, not put her down." With a five second pause, Maxine laughed and said, "Child, please, anyways, on to the next line up of dirt." "Alright, what is it?" I drooled at the mouth for more. "Baseball player, Tony has been taking steroids and basketball player Jake, better known as fridge, got Rachel from the cheerleading team pregnant." "What? Wow! When? I'm in total shock about Jake. He is so cute."   "I got a friend that works at the CVS, and he saw Rachel getting a pregnancy test. That can only mean one thing, the girl is pregnant. Oh yeah, one last scoop for the night. I've been personally hearing people say your mom gives too much work. I even heard some say that she's the Anti-Christ of high school. I don't know girl, you might want to look into that mess." "Wow, saying my mother is the Anti-Christ is a real low blow. The blow is low; I can feel my stomach flipping. That's just totally stupid." "Girl, it's going to be alright, just some haters hating on your mother."   "Yeah, so what should   I   do   about   that?" "Nothing. If you try to do something it will only make it worse. Your mom can handle herself. Not like they got a death threat out there on her. Your little friend Sonya is the only one I'm worried about."   I guess I'm worried about her too.   "Precious you still there?" Maxine yelled me out of my daydreaming.   "Yeah." My heart rate went up a few notches.   "Well you got a little quiet on the phone, did I say something wrong?"   "No, you good, you just got me thinking," she really has me thinking.   "About your   friend,   huh?"   Maxine   muttered. "A little bit," I'm lying I'm thinking about this

Sonya girl a lot.   "Hey girl, I know it's hard, but you just have to let go of some people. Light and darkness can't go together." "Tell me about it." Thinking about our conversation, how dark are we to talk about people like that?   We   have   to   do   better. "What's that supposed to mean?" Maxine took offense.   "Nothing, it's just that you're right about that light and darkness stuff." Maxine is the last one to talk about light and darkness. All of that gossiping she does, it's a wonder that I'm friends with her. I guess maybe our friendship is based on pure entertainment, and she is pretty popular around the school. Maybe Maxine represents the side of me that I could be. Maybe Maxine is the hidden me. I guess that's what makes me beautifully ugly. Lord, forgive me of my transgressions, for I know not what I do.

UNREST

"So what should I do, Precious? Should I kill him?" "No, Sonya, of course not. The Bible says do not kill. You need to find a way to turn your father in and get your mother and younger brothers out. You need help, Sonya." "So you think your God can help me?" She said with a look of grave displeasure. "Yes, exactly, God can help do anything. He's not just my God, but he's ultimately your God too. God puts people in certain places and seasons to help us as well; people such as counselors, police officers, and non-profit organizations. You don't have to be in that mess! Please let go and let God." "Your God let all this happen to us; He could have stopped this before it started. What is he going to do? If he hasn't done anything all these years, what makes you so sure He's going to help now?" Sonya huffed and puffed, accusing God of things in which He did not do. "Nothing honestly, nothing makes me sure. But, I am sure that he's a just and righteous God. My daddy is a Deacon, and he taught me a lot about the things of God. I must confess, I'm still learning and don't know a lot, but I do know that God loves me and he loves you too." As soon as I mentioned God loving Sonya, I could tell that I hit a tender spot; a pinch of water rolled from under her eyes. She was touched, she needs to feel loved, and she needs Jesus.   "Well, Precious, I can't promise you that I'll do something about this God thing, but I am going to do something about my dad." She   lowered   her   head. "Please, don't do anything crazy, Sonya." I pleaded with her.   "Are you calling me crazy, Precious?"   She   quickly   took   offense. "No, I wasn't calling you crazy. I just said; don't do anything crazy, okay?"   `

"Yeah. Whatever!"   She rolled her eyes at me. "What's that supposed to mean?" I felt shafted. "I'm not perfect, Precious. I got a lot of things to deal with right now, and I don't quite know how to deal with them. Everything you said sounds pretty good, but it also has to make sense to me." "I'm here to help you, Sonya. I'm really, really here to help you, Sonya. I will pray for you, okay?" "I'm afraid it's too late." She finally picked her head up.   "It's never too late. Why are you talking like that, girl?" She began to scare me and left me unsure of what to do or say. "Because," She slightly shrugged her shoulders back, looking like an innocent little child. "Because what?" I quickly responded as a desperate   gesture   for   an   answer. "Nobody loves me; my mother and father never say they love me. They never give me a hug. Nobody cares about me, and this world is full of hate. These people are full of crap. People gossip and act a fool all the time. I guess I'm supposed to be this naïve person all my life; being abused, hated, and laughed at, teachers disappointing me, and boys not wanting me. Nobody loves me, nobody, nobody ever did. And no one ever will. She looked down with utter frustration, a speckled tear formed under her left eye; she's hurt so bad that even pain doesn't seem to recognize her. "But I love you, Sonya, and God loves you. I, I just don't know what else I can say about that. I want to be your friend; I want to help see you through this. I just want you to be happy." "Happiness is the thought that I've been living for over the past sixteen years of my life. Happiness is just that, a thought. How could I be happy, when I've never experienced a day of it? Are you happy now?" She turned away from me. "No, why would I be happy to hear of your unhappiness? I cry for you; I want you to be free." This is deep, real deep. "I cry for me, too." She sobbed like a little girl lost in the world. Patting her feet in silence she walked away, smaller and smaller she became, as she walked down the hallway and exited the school. I don't know where she was going; school is still in session. But whatever she's going to do, and wherever she's going, she's obviously made up her mind. I've tried to help her the best way I could; maybe, I'd go to the counselor and tell her about this problem. This problem has gotten way beyond me now. She needs some help; her family needs help before it's too late.

"Precious, what do you want, and who do you want to speak with," the secretary in the main office asked. "I need to speak to my counselor about some issues." Chills ran all the way up to the tip of my skin, the likeness of goose bumps and fear superseded my imagination. I'm afraid for Sonya, most importantly, I'm afraid for what she may do. "Why don't you just talk to your mom, she works here, too?" This lady is about to get on my nerves. "Well, it's very important that I speak with my counselor." "She's busy at the moment; you're going to have to wait just like everyone else. You think you got special treatment just because your mom works here. I don't think so. There will be a twenty minute wait, by the way; you can take a number and sit down. Thank you." Oh no, she didn't just insult me like that! Now I see what my brother Justin went through in his days of high school and mother working at the same school. These people are idiots, and so rude. I'll wait though; I'll wait, this is very important. "Thank you!" She got some nerves. I hope Sonya doesn't do anything stupid, and I hope Maxine was so wrong about her. The last thing I need is Maxine pointing back at me saying I told you so, like she does the majority of the time. Speaking of Maxine, here she comes rolling in the office.

"Hey girl, what are you doing in here? Are you pregnant?" Maxine took a look at my cheeks and then my stomach. I guess I am a little swollen up in the chin from all that drama with Sonya. "No Maxine, of course you know I'm not pregnant, never been touched." She didn't even blink when I said it.   "Girl, you know I'm kidding. So what are you in here for?" She's ready to find some dirt. That girl could sniff a weasel out of his underground home with the right information. I must give it to her; she's smart and cunning at the same time. "Private matters which do not concern you." I gave her the cold treatment, couldn't risk any more damage being done to Sonya.   "I know why, you in here about that Sonya chick, right? Good decision."   How the heck does she know? She must have spies all over Morning Glory High   School. "I'm not telling, ouch" my knuckles cracked. "You just gave it away; it's cool though Precious. I'm   not   telling   anybody!" That's a lie, just as sure as the ocean holds water. Maxine can't hold a secret to save her life. "Okay, so what are you in here for?" I took a mental picture of her chin and stomach the same way she looked at me. Who knows, she could be pregnant, or   at   least   pregnant   with   gossip.

"Girl my allergies been bothering me. I figured maybe my counselor can tell me what to do about that." Yeah right.   "Maxine, you don't need to see a counselor; you need to see the   school   nurse." "Yeah, but I find out most of the dirt going on around the school right here. This office is the core of things happening around here. From what teacher slept with what student, to what talk show is always being played in Mr. Vonclad's class. Girl, it's so much news in this office, I could start a daily soap."   She's not lying about that part, she could probably pass for the Wendy Williams type, dishing out daily news and hot topics. "Maxine, you need to quit. Go back to class; I bet there is nothing wrong with your allergies." I did a double take just to make sure she was telling the truth, smiling hard in the process, trying not to laugh   my   behind   off.   She's   lying. "You right, girl, but I got to keep up with the hot things going around school." She looked frustrated, maybe she feels guilty for me peeping her game, or the fact that she finally revealed one of her sources for gossip.   "Are you paid to do this," I asked with the utmost level of nosiness.   "Sometimes I get paid like a hundred dollars, when I broke the news about Tony the   base   ball   player;   I   got   paid   girl." "What? Who's paying you?" Wow, this girl gets more   and   more   unbelievable. "Girl, I can't tell you that. Let's just say I have plenty of clients, plenty of repeat customers, and that's confidential." "Ok, well is that legal?" She's about to get herself in trouble. "Of course, I'm just like any newspaper or magazine delivering the news. They pay people like me to give them what the people want to hear." "So, are you working for a magazine?" Let me know where I can sign up. "Of course not Precious, Morning Glory High School ain't that important. But let's just say this; there are plenty of girls at this school and some guys who don't mind paying me to find out if their lover is cheating." "Precious Lewis, I'm looking for Precious Lewis please." The counselor walked from the back looking for me. "She calling my name Maxine; I'll talk to you later," She looked a litte disappointed. "Good luck, I hope your friend gets some help," Maxine sighed, and then at the turn of events, she abruptly moved away from me towards the office door, swinging each hip in the process. "Precious Lewis, where are you?" The counselor called out, obviously more frustrated with me for not responding to her. "I'm right here, ma'am." "Well, come on; wouldn't want you to lose your turn." I grabbed my bags and followed her in the office. "So what is this about, Precious? I see you wrote urgent and confidential. Is everything ok with you?"

"Yes, yes everything is okay with me. I just got this friend who I'm afraid is not okay." "Continue," she coached me on, looking at me with such a severe and loving demeanor. I felt so warm inside; she makes me feel comfortable. "Okay, I Just thought that I would've been able to help her, but I feel that the problem she is facing is over my head." "What's the problem? It's ok to tell me," she demanded. Still loving, but clearly a little agitated. With a quick change in posture she relaxed a tad bit. I guess she figured she didn't want to discourage me, or prevent me from expressing her mind by the hurried tone in her voice. "She's talking about killing her father," was the most critical words I could have blurted out. I didn't care anymore, it needed to be said. "Who's talking about killing their father?" She began to look at me with a strange amount of fear. "Sonya." This is hard. "Sonya who?" The counselor keeps digging, and I kept stalling. "Sonya Moten." I finally caved in; it's really the right thing to do. "Yes, I'm very aware of her. She came in here the other day, talking about killing her father. So you are the girl she wrote that letter to? How come you didn't tell us about this earlier?" She took a deep breath and then looked me straight in the eyes. Now I'm scared. "I was afraid; she told me not to tell anyone. And her letter didn't actually say she was going to kill

him. She asked if she should kill him."
"Well, to your benefit, we've already alerted the police about this, and they have put a restraining order on Sonya. She can't be within one thousand feet of her father. Right now, the paper work is in process to put her in a foster home. Currently, she should be in the care of her grandmother."
"Her father has been abusing them. Why does she have the restraining order?"
"I can't speak on behalf of the police. She did speak on something about abuse, but she did not identify to me who was abusing who or whatever. So yes, right now it's best that you also keep a distance from her too. She seemed very fragile when she came in, and we don't know where she is right now." "I know, she walked out the school about an hour ago."
"Where did she go?" She reached for a pen and paper. "I don't know; my guess is as good as yours. She said she didn't feel loved and said she was going to do something. She never told me that she spoke to you. I was trying to encourage her to speak to someone like you."
"Hold up a minute, I need to call the police," she panicked. "Okay." So that's how Maxine knows what she knows about Sonya. Sonya was in here. I feel so stupid now. The counselor got to dialing." Yes, I'm calling from Morning Glory High School; I'm one of the counselors here. Is Officer Gonzalez available?"
"No, he's on the scene of a homicide," the dis-

patcher on the line reported. That's not good. Shocked and frustrated, "okay, is there someone there that I can talk to?" "No, but I can leave a message, counselor." The dispatcher hurriedly told her. "I have a student who plans to kill her father; she left the school about an hour ago. No one knows where she is. I was hoping you all could get an officer to the home." "Oh, sorry ma'am, I'll dispatch someone out right now. What is the address, and what's the student's name?" "I don't quite know the address, but the student's name is Sonya Moten. You all should have the address in your files," she leaned back gasping for air, extreme panic takes over. "Okay, I found it. Someone should be there in five minutes. In the mean time, I suggest you call a lock down on the school. We'll have a couple of officers dispatched to your school as well." The dispatcher tried to make sense of it all. "Okay." the counselor hung up with the dispatcher and frantically picked up her notes. "I'm sorry, Precious, I have to go and get this announcement through. You may need to stay here as a witness to this case. I need to go over to the principal's office. In the meantime, you need to call your parents and tell them what's happening." She worked up a sweat. "Well, my mother works here." I'm surprised she didn't know that; everyone else seems to.

"Even better Precious; is she a teacher or custodian?" She rose from her chair. "She's a teacher." I gave her the look. "Call her classroom, and then return to my office, immediately. You have to stay here as a witness." She left the office and zoomed into the principal's office a few steps away. Lord, I pray that nothing bad has happened. I pray that it's not too late. I'm scared. And then the Lord spoke to me and said, "Be strong and of good courage. This battle is not yours, for it is mine. Be the victor I've made you to be, and truth and happiness will come to you." Just as quickly as I called on Him, He said not another word. Seems like He didn't answer my question, but He did give me hope, and right now I guess that's all I need.

"Precious, I came as soon as they called me, are you okay?" She looked at me with grave concern. How can I tell my mother all that's been going on these past two days? "Yes, mother, I'm fine. I'm just pretty frustrated right now, but I'm happy to see you." I really am happy to see her, I should have brought this situation to her, yesterday, and then I wouldn't have to go through this mess that I'm going through now. What if someone gets hurt? Then, it would be all my fault. Life throws its blows at you right when you least expect it too. "Your father is on his way; tell me what happened." Now I have to tell her everything, huhh… "Well, there is this girl name Sonya that I met the other day." Here I am stalling again. "Sonya, who?" just like the counselor, my mother wants the last name. I just hope this is my last time telling this story. "What? You know her too?" I felt shocked and embarrassed. "I might, what is her last name?" My mother insisted, looking at me straight in the eyes like my counselor did. Maybe all adults are like this. "Moten, her name is Sonya Moten," I spilled the beans again. "Oh, her." My mother rolled her eyes at me. "What? What do you know about her?" How come I feel so left in the dark? Who is this Sonya Moten? It seems like I know nothing about her. It seems like she was not completely honest with me. Maxine is going to have a field day. "For starters, my daughter, the girl told me right to my face that I give too much homework. I felt so embarrassed, because it reminded me of that teacher Justin had in elementary school. I know how mad I was at that lady for giving him all that work. Secondly, home girl reported me to the principal. I was in utter shock." "You are talking about Dr. Adams?" My eyes just about bulged out of their sockets; my mother exchanged the same intensity. "Yes, her first day here, she gets a complaint about me giving too much homework." "You mean the lady who's the principal now is the lady who used to drive you and Justin crazy in Tallahassee is now here?" "Yes."

My mother looked as if she was ready to scream. "Why?" I'm ready to scream. "She got transferred to help with these unruly kids; it's a war in this place. As a matter of fact, your father and I have been thinking about putting you in private school. But I'll hold that thought for later. So, what's going on with you and this Sonya girl?" Should I tell her or should I keep this secret between myself, Sonya and the counselor. That's right, the counselor knows. I guess it's not much of a secret now. The only real secret is the fact that I hardly know a thing about this Sonya girl. I don't know her favorite likes and dislikes. I don't even know what boy she might have a crush on. This really sucks, now my mother has to get involved like this is another episode of Law and Order SVU. "Sonya told me that she was thinking about killing her abusive father, and I kind of took it for granted. I feel bad now, because she left the school, and there is no telling what she did when she got home." Just when I thought that my mother would fuss till her face turned purple, which takes a long time for black folks, my mother was a comforter. "It's going to be alright, baby; it's going to be alright. Your father will be here any minute now to take you home to get some rest." "But the counselor lady said to stay here as a witness when the cops come," I whined like a little girl, wanting my mother's sympathy, hoping she could get me home sooner than my father could make it here. "Don't worry about the cops, baby; your father and I will handle them. You are under the age of eighteen so they can't question you without our permission, anyway." "Well, I hope daddy is bringing something to eat too, because I'm hungry. I'm really, really hungry." "You can pick up some food on the way home. In the mean time, you make sure you get some rest; we have a long couple of days before us." I guess my mother is right about that part. We do have a long couple of days. Hopefully they are for the good.

SONYA MOTEN

There has to be more to life than this, for what I see and how I live is the evidence of filth masquerading as the law. My father or better yet, step father hates me; he shows no love and could careless about mercy. If there was any rhyme or reason for this then maybe, just maybe I should kill myself. What will it solve if I shoved a gun to my head and pulled the trigger? What reward will I gain by killing my step-father? He will then be seen as a hero, a mortar of sorts and then his name will go in the history books for ever. I don't want that, I don't want people to remember him. I want people to remember me. It's me they should re-member, Sonya Moten, the little girl that tried to protect her younger brothers. The girl that tried to help her stupid mother, I tried to warn her about marrying that guy, but she couldn't see through his cunning and evil ways if I took an ice-pick and picked every scummy lie and mis-truth that the man had ever spoken. Then Precious, oh Precious, as much as I admire and am grateful for her taking up for me the other day, she has it all wrong. I don't know who's warped her mind, but there is no such thing as god, at least not one that I know. It's just not right for a god to sit there and watch the abuse happen and not do one thing about it. If there was a god that called himself to be just and committed to his people, then I'd rather make my bed in hell, at least I know I'd be happier there knowing that the hell I experience on this earth right now will be the same hell that id be use to in the afterlife. Oh what should I do what should I do? I have already skipped class so I'm sure they are calling the cops ort something. I never imagined that I would be in a situation like this, with a ten inch knife in my back pocket made with grooves that could gut a fish on one lunge; somebody is going to die today. Somebody is going to die to day! I deserved better, I deserved to grow up like the other kids, happy, well-nourished and loved. Doesn't everyone deserve to be loved? Doesn't everyone deserve a second chance? Why not me? Why not me? If there is a god, at least the god that Precious claims she serves, do you hear me? Do you hear my request, you god of the sky. Do you even know my name? Have you thought about my beautiful green eyes and stretched lashes? Have you counted the strands of my luscious black hair? Have you even looked into my freckled face lately to see the pain that I harbor inside? Are you willing and able to help me, the god of Precious. You say that you are god, but why can't I hear you? Why don't I feel the same way Precious does?

What is your agenda? What kind of laughs are you getting out of my ugly situation? What's in it for you, hunh?   "Shh…Hush my child. I have heard your cries and understand your plea. For the answers you seek are not unreasonable, for they are common amongst my people. And as far as your hair and eyes go, I knew you before you were born. I remember when you were just a little baby kicking and moving in your mother's womb, ready to get out and explore the world. Sonya, I remember when you wet your first diaper, your mother screamed because she did not know what to do as a first time mother. But she wiped your little butt and made you clean and whole again. I remember when you use to look up to the stars and count each star searching for a planet amongst the stars, looking for some signs of anything that was greater than you. Sonya my daughter, I just want you to know that I am God, the one and only true God, after me, there is no other. I love you in-spite of however you may feel towards me."   But how do I know that it's you talking to me and not just me talking to myself, my mother said that I've been going   crazy   and   stuff   lately. "You know because you know, I want to share with you a little secret that was told between you and your mother. Your mother promised that she never told that secret to anybody but you, but the secret brought her so much pain and heartache. When your mother was sixteen, she shared with you that you weren't truly her first child. When she was sixteen she had an abortion. Now although she never gave the child a name, I named her Heather and she is sitting amongst the millions of children here in heaven. Heather is your sister and she is quite a bundle of joy, she knows her scriptures backwards and forwards and she knows the struggles that you have been through with your father." You mean my step-father, right God. "He is your father; any man that takes upon himself to raise and support the children of the house is a father to you. No he is not your biological father, but he is your father. The man that has put a roof over your head and clothes on your back, no matter how hard you try to hate him, he still is the man of the house. None of my children who serve me call me step-father God. They simply call me father, I provide the same things and more that your earthly father does, but few appreciate what I actually do because they rarely get to see it unless they are looking through their spiritual eyes. So you see Sonya, what you accuse me of not doing is only an example of your immaturity and unwillingness to really know who I Am. Today is your day to take my hand in love and worship me the one and only true God. Today is your day to call me father, for I see and I know everything, every little secret, every little mistake. Will you come to me with love and a heart quipped for forgiveness of your father."

No, I can't I can't and I never will forgive that bastard. He's a lying crook. This is all in my head. You aren't real. This must be my imagination. I can never forgive him; he tried to strangle me one day. I'm going to kill him! He's going to die; it's going to either be him or me. This day will be his last day, his last opportunity to breathe. "Sonya, you and your father's blood is for me to decide on. That decision does not belong to you. For I am God, and you are looking to do my job." No, you've had an opportunity to do your job. And you've failed, get out of my head. Leave me alone, the decision has already been made!

LIES WITH DEATH

"Sonya Moten was a good woman. She was probably a woman after God's own heart.   The kids at school would say that Sonya was very gifted and creative. She was too young to die. Sonya was one of God's children, and she lived her short life the way that God would have seen it." This pastor is telling a bunch of lies. Sonya didn't know God. Sonya hated God. I can't wait until this service is over. I may need to change the eulogy.

And the preacher continues to preach describing Sonya as, "a passionate woman who had faith like a mustard seed. She was her mother's pride and her father's angel. Her brothers, oh her two brothers looked up to her with joy and praises, this day, this time; she's up in heaven singing praises to our God." I'm about to puke. I can't take any more of these lies. Why doesn't someone stand up to the Pastor and make him tell the truth; somebody,   anybody!
"Yes, she has committed suicide, but the burdens

of life have been removed from her soul. She's free now, ladies and gentlemen, she's free! No more shackles, no more pain, she's free, and she's free indeed!" The pastor continues on, moving the church into tears. "Excuse me, Mrs. Moten, you mind if I speak to you for a second?" I just have to speak to this lady; somebody needs to tell the truth around here. "Sure, you're the girl that spoke with her in her final days." She gave me a questionable glance. "Yes, that's me, my name is Precious." "That's cute; my daughter's name is Precious." "That's funny; Sonya never mentioned she had a sister." Now I'm really taken back. "She probably didn't mention it, because she's a new born. Precious is only a couple of months old. So, Precious, what do you want from me?" "The truth," I said, boldly looking into her healthy green eyes. "Ok, what do you want to know?" Her eyes widened and breathing became a little heavier than before. "Is it true that your husband is abusing you?" My knuckles cracked after asking this question. "Absolutely not, do you see a blue eye or scratch on me anywhere? I'll even show you my back if you like; and honey I'm not wearing makeup." She certainly didn't look as frail as Sonya described and she sounds pretty forward to me. "Listen honey, my daughter Sonya was suffering from a crisis of identity. She made up countless stories to the police and counselors, and she has literally put our family through Hell and back. Everyday there was an officer checking on my husband. My husband can't go to work without being followed. All of us were being photographed; it just became a nightmare. Sonya is my child from a previous marriage. Ever since that divorce, Sonya has made up little worlds and stories for herself. I even heard that she made up names for herself too. We think that a lot of what she was going through was between Post Traumatic Stress and the doctor concluding that she was bipolar. Things in our home didn't start heating up till she was threatening to kill my husband repeatedly, about a month ago. At that point the police put a restraining order against her and were ready to send her to the crazy house. I said 'no,' because I wanted her to be able to have a normal life. So, I sent her to her grandmother's place a few blocks down. It was tough, but it was either that or the crazy house. So, here we are now, talking about Sonya. Now, she can rest in peace. I loved her so much, but I can't say I didn't see something like this coming sooner or later. It was either going to be her life or my husband's life. She chose to take her life. Like I said, she was bipolar; no telling what else she plotted to do." "Thank you Mrs. Moten, thank you." Wow, that is something; no wonder there were so many lies. I guess Sonya never had a true chance in this life. I hope she found Jesus before she gave up the ghost.

MORNING GLORY HIGH SCHOOL

A warm feeling of guilt, shame, and shock covered Morning Glory High School. People are looking depressed, saddened, and in despair, over the suicide of Sonya. Wow, I didn't know that this many people knew her; more or less cared about her. Even the flag is at half staff for her. The hallways are quiet and I could barely see a dry eye. Who was this girl? Things seem to get stranger and stranger the more I hear about her.   In the cafeteria, all I could hear are the student's personal encounters with her. There was this dude that spoke about her well; she helped him in math. She's not even good in math.   Was she living some sort of double life I don't know about? She was bipolar. Another guy spoke on how well she hit a baseball. Two girls at the same table were crying all over the table. Water and snot was dripping everywhere. But me, little me, I seemed like just a small fraction in her life. When I thought that I was the main one in her life for the short period of time that I got to know her. Everyone knew about the letter by now, and they knew how she met me in her final days. But many were uninterested in what I had to say. All they wanted to do is mope and cry. I wonder, I just wonder where they were when she needed their help. I'm going to my mother's class, I don't feel so good. Something inside of me just makes me want to scream. I feel so heavy inside; so much junk, so much drama within these last couple of days. Oh, now my head is hurting. "Ahhh---!" I yelled to the top of my lungs in the cafeteria. Everyone ran out, everyone ducked for cover. They must have thought I had a gun. But then I ran out, and all eyes were on me. I felt worse than I felt before. For the first time in a long time, I discovered a dark side of me. All the attention was on Sonya, when I really wanted the attention to be on me. Why couldn't the boys cry for me? Why couldn't the boys talk about how I played baseball? Wanting all the attention, all the glory, is what makes me beautifully ugly. Here you have my girlfriend who I just met, die because of suicide; but yet I wanted everyone to care about me. Was I that wrong God? Was I that naïve? I'm just a seventeen year old girl at Morning Glory High School. Why can't more people look at me? The old heads always talk about getting their flowers before they die. Why can't I get a little bit of love around here? "Precious, Precious, Precious," said the voice of God, so softly. "You will face vast amounts of troubles in the days to come. Be on your guard, for the enemy wants to destroy you. But I shall put a veil of protection over you. He may be able to touch your body, but he will not be able to touch your soul." "What is that suppose to mean?" And as sure as I spoke, he was silent. Not another word uttered from his presence. God is so awesome, so rich, and so holy. I can't believe he loves me. I understand everything he said; except for the enemy being able to touch my body but not my soul. If my daddy has something to say about it, he'll make sure no one lays a finger on me. "Precious what are you doing here?" My mother looked at me strangely, but the stillness in her eyes helped me to realize that she knew why. "I don't feel so good mother." She doesn't have a clue how bad I feel.   "Well take a seat to the back of the class. The students are currently writing a one page essay on suicide causes, concerns, and remedies. Would you care to join us?"

"No, I'm cool. I'll just be back here listening to you." Now my mother is in on the Sonya drama. So   not   cool. "Okay, suit yourself." She picked up the paper she was working on before I came in to her class. My mother placed the paper down, "Do I have any volunteers to read their input on suicide?" She paused and looked around the room. "No one what-so-ever wants to read?" Before my mother could lift her finger to choose a student, the girl three desks in front of me decided to stand up and give her reasoning. "Well I'm glad you stood up Claritha." "Mrs. Lewis, I uh…uh, kind of did it different from what you asked. I did it where it kind of like talks about my personal accounts with the thoughts of suicide and depression." My mother looked at me for a brief second, "That's okay, Claritha, as long as you are comfortable with sharing your personal experience with the class its okay with me." I guess she wanted to make sure I was comfortable with listening. "Yes, I'm comfortable Mrs. Lewis." The girl looked nervous as a bat on a sunny day. "You may begin, class please try not to be rude and definitely don't choose to judge her for whatever she has to say. Go ahead Claritha." My mother comforted her. "Hi class, as you know my name is Claritha. I know it seems kind of hard to talk about suicide and depression. But suicide is one of the leading causes of death amongst us teenagers." Please don't cry, please don't cry. Ok she's crying. Game is over; serious face is done. "You can stop right there Claritha, it's ok." My mother interrupts. "No," with raised eyebrows and wet cheeks "this thing is way more important than me. We are talking life or death here, people. I just feel a lot of pain and hurt by some of the things that went on. Much love goes out to our dear sister Sonya, she will be missed. For years I've grown up believing that I was a no-body; not good enough for anybody. Not good enough for my parents, my friends, neighbors and even boyfriends. Yeah, I grew up with both my parents, yet I felt as lonely as an only child. There ain't no one to blame when the bathroom cabin breaks, the sink over fills, or the room is dirty. Only one that I was able to blame was myself. Nevertheless, I realized that a lot of the things I broke were to attract attention from my parents. My mother is a doctor and my dad is the C.E.O of a Fortune 500 company. It's been like they don't even care about me. They don't care about my needs, my desires, only what's best for them in the end. Only what makes their name look good is all that they were concerned about." She shook her head, and paused for a quick breather, everyone else was mute, and not a crack of boredom filled their faces.

Clairtha continued with another round of tears, "Don't get me wrong, they are good parents. They provide a roof over my head, clothes on my back, and good food to eat. All of that is good, but I wanted more. I want to see them more; I want my dad to come home at night and kiss me on the cheeks and tell me he loves me. I know he loves me, but I didn't see him enough for him to show me how. I want more than money from him. I want a promise and commitment to tend to my needs. Yeah I get money, but what is it worth if I don't have happiness?" "I don't know Claritha, I don't know." My mother said, with tears blushing down her cheeks. Somebody has to break this morbid mood. Lawd knows I don't want to cry too. Claritha continued on with her story once more "I, I just felt that life was not worth it; time to kick the bucket. All that consumed the back of my mind was, my parents don't love me, boyfriends don't want me, and teachers don't pay attention to me in school. But you know what? I know that it's the devil's foolishness trying to wreak havoc on my mind. One of my counselors from the church calls it the spirit of suicide. And I tell you this; I bind that spirit of suicide in the name of Jesus Christ of Nazareth, who died in the flesh for my sins. I beseech you; you foul spirit in the name of Jesus, Jesus Christ! Amen." "Alright Claritha, thank you for sharing such a personal encounter with suicide for the class. What's one last thing, Claritha, that you can tell the class, for those who are thinking about suicide?" "I would say to really, really pray. Dig deep within yourself to see the beauty which God has placed in you. I'm not going to lie; you're not always going to have good days. But at least you can remind yourself of the good times, and the good which God has placed in your life." "Thank you very, very much, Claritha. Class let's give her a round of applause. She deserves the best from you." My mother looked back at me as if she wants to tell me something. Oops looks like she does.   "Precious will you please get my purse out of my car? Thanks."   Before I even have a chance to say anything else, she's talking about thanks. That's the problem with adults; they ask if you can do something for them with no intention of hearing a response. But that's okay, wait till I hit eighteen, it's all over then.   "Oh, mother, let me hold the keys." I take a quick journey to her desk, by this time the mood in the classroom was a little better, although Clairtha looked as if she wanted to leave on the first train coming. You never know what's going on inside of someone's mind. Claritha is one of the most beautiful and blessed looking girls' here at Glory High, to find out that she's been depressed and suicidal, well that's just above my pay grade.   "Here you go, Precious; I'll see you in a little bit. And straighten up that attitude."

JUSTIN IS HOME

"What are you doing home right now? It's only a few weeks into the full semester." My mother questioned Justin, my big brother, who means the world to me.   "I quit, mama, I quit!" Oh no, Justin did not just say the 'q' word. "You what?" My mother looked at him with utter surprise and suspicion; she nearly fainted at the news.

"I quit, I'm tired of not making any progress up there in college; just ain't for me." I am in total disbelief. I told my brother about messing around with them girls.   "So what do you think your father is going to say about this?" My mother shook her head back and forth, shaking her back into reality along the way.   "It doesn't matter because I'm a man now. I don't have to listen to him. I got my own set of rules." Some girl must've really gotten him hooked. I never heard him talk to my mother like that. He done said quite a thing in his day, but not like that. "Excuse me, Justin, what did you just say to me?" She quickly placed herself in front of Justin, her hand held forward, willing and ready to back hand him.   "I am a man! I don't have time for dad to lecture me about school. School for me is just not cool. I hate it! I hate it!" My mother tried to reason with him, "Is it because of your major? What's the problem?" She sulked. "I don't think it has anything to do with my major, mama.   I   just   think   I   need   a   break." "You just had a break!" Her voice rang out as loud as the soprano section, she wasn't going to take 'no' for an answer.   "I don't know, ma, I don't know." He looked down at his feet, dreads mangled up, and lime-green Polo shirt pressed fresh. The little boy I once knew and cherished as my brother has now come to set his place   amongst   men. "Well, son, go wash up and get ready for dinner. I am happy to see you, of course, but not necessarily under these circumstances. I'd rather just give you a hug without having to worry about the other stuff."   "Where's my   little   sister   at?" "She should be back there playing video games, getting her fingernails polished, or something. I don't know Justin; just go back there and see about her."   "Okay." He trips over a cord in the kitchen as he heads to my room. I sort of have a double edged sword type of feeling with my brother right now. I would love to have him here on a few weekends talking about college life, but on the other side of that sword, he's not in

college. He decided to leave before he even asked mama and daddy about it; even though they were going to say 'no.' He could have at least asked for their opinions to make a wiser decision. I don't know, but I'm going to love him regardless. Here he   comes.
"Precious, how are you doing baby girl?" He walked in with his five foot eleven swagger, this brother of mine done changed, and I bet them girls up   in   Atlanta   done   turned   him   out. "Justin I miss you, I love you. Boy you done put on a few pounds, and you got a little taller. No won-der you have them girls all over you. You look good   big   brother,   you   look   good." "Well you know, sis, I do what I do. You don't look so   bad   yourself."   He   chuckled. "So   you   like   my   hair?" "Yeah, it's different, but I like it." He smiled, just to see the warmth of my brother's smile at this mo-ment   is   worth   a   million   bucks. "I am so glad you are home. It's not that often we get to see you."   "Yeah, I'll be here for a little while. I sort of kind of quit college for the moment. I don't necessarily understand it all, but right now it's the decision I just had to make. Things are going a little crazy for me right now. School ain't the way it used to be, Precious." "What about the band? The band director won't like that, and you got a scholarship. You mean to tell me you are willing to leave all that behind? "I don't know, I'm not really sure; but I'm sure our

father is going to be pissed." He looked at me with those troubled eyes. "Yeah, I heard mama talking about that." "You mean to tell me you knew about this the whole time? If you weren't a girl, I'd be beating you up." He pulled me into him, and then with one quick sting to the neck, he popped me gently. "Ouch...Don't get mad at me Justin; you are the one who dropped out of school." Mama's voice overshadowed what I was about to say next. "Dinner's ready, wash up children." "We will finish this later Precious." Yep, right at the dinner table. Watch, he'll see daddy's going to give him a piece of his mind.

"Ooh-- ma, I love the baked beans; taste like you done put your foot down in that pot," Justin egged on my mother's ego. "I knew you would miss my home cooking up there with those college kids. College kids do not know how to cook. You all would cook some noodles and ground beef, then call it cuisine." Justin defended his collegiate recipes, "better than eating canned sausages." "Yeah, go figure," my dad jumped into the conversation; that's when the whole table got quiet. "Hey, you all could keep talking; don't stop because of me. I'm just a tired angry black man right now. Who wouldn't want to talk to me?" My father was begging for us to feel sorry for his feelings. "Rodney."

My mother whipped him a glance. "What?" My father said with a disgruntled look, not sure if he was more disturbed that she called his name in the middle of chewing on the fat of the rib tip, or because he was just annoyed. "Go ahead and say what you have to say; no need of beating around the bush." She said sternly, opening a can of worms which I knew were to be released soon. I smell trouble. "Well I ain't beating around the bush; I just don't have much if anything to say." His face dropped, and then he dug back into the ribs and sipping the beans as if they were a homemade glass of Kool-Aid. "Well you should; your son just dropped out of college. Don't you think that's worth speaking on?" "The boy is a grown man, Sandra; there is little to nothing I can do to make him go back. It all has to be done on God's timing. His grades ain't been all that great anyway. So maybe this is the best decision for now." "So what? He's just going to be staying at the house doing nothing?" My mother cringed with a big frown on her face. Justin and I are trading glances at each other as our parents hash it out. "No, I can get him a job doing construction, that way he could see what life is like in the real world. He'll see how hard it is to work around here without a college education." "That sounds like a plan. Justin, are you down for that?" My mother smiled, satisfied that a plan were to be into place to save my brother from the streets.   "Do I have a choice?" Both of my parents rushed to a response, just like the love bugs you see dancing around the cars, they both said, "No" as if they were joined to the hips happily in love with their decision. "Okay, when do I start?" Justin quickly humbled himself for the sake of argument and getting kicked   out   of   the   house. "Next Monday." My father joyfully told him, as if Justin just signed up for some secret mission that only   my   dad   knows   about. "Alright, that's cool. Can I be excused?" Justin looked over to my parents and me.   "Yes, of course you can. Precious you stay put." My mother glanced at me as if I just revealed that I was pregnant or something. This can't be good. But what did I do?   "O-kay, mother," I slurred, anticipating   the   worst. "Have a good night Justin." My parents cheered him on, my father looking a little aggravated and my   mother   clearly   stressed. "Okay, ma; alright pops; I'll see you tomorrow." Justin winked at me as he strolled on down the hallway   into   his   room. "My mother began to talk. "Oh, Precious, you see that? That's an example of failure. Your father and I have invested too much of our time and money into Justin for him to just up and quit like that. It's depressing."   My father interrupted, "Baby, don't look at it like that. Look at it like this--." I know that whatever he's about to say will make a whole lot of sense. "Look at it like this, baby; he will have to live with his choices. We are no longer privileged to make decisions for him. He must make decisions for himself. The furthest we realize that the Justin we birthed is not the same Justin that just left this table, we will understand better what it means to let go and let God." "But I, I don't want to let go. I want my baby back. I want the Justin that I use to rock and cradle at nights when he wet the bed. He was my comforter when you were away, kept me and consoled when I'd cry because you were gone. That's the Justin I want back, right now." My mother's eyes weaken with moisture. "I know you do, baby, I know you do. But growing up is just a part of the cycle of life; which we cannot control. We couldn't control it when we were getting older. If it was up to me, I'd be nineteen again."

"Tell me about it." My mother softly patted her eyes with the napkin which was sitting next to her vastly decorated platter. "God has a funny way of teaching us lessons. Many of the failures I've committed I can see them in Justin. What's up with that?" My father nodded his head then looked towards me for an answer. I don't have an answer, I don't even know what he's talking about. "I don't know baby; ask the big man upstairs." My mother coached him. "I don't think that God and I are on speaking terms right now." His whole demeanor changed. "Why? What did you do?" She said with raised eye brows and clinched teeth. "I cussed this old lady out in the parking lot. I had a bad day, and the hag was moving too slow." "Rodney," my mother whined. "I know baby, I shouldn't have done it." She returned her glance, this time to get ter a deeper more intimate look at her burly clean shaven husband. She could see the disappointment in his eyes, and the wear and tear of age peeking under his eyelids." Well all you have to do is ask the Lord for forgiveness. You've committed much worse crimes than that." "Yeah, I just got to get around to it," my father replied with guilt and shame written with bold italics across his face.

"Do it now," my mother commanded. "God's grace is sufficient. Who knows, you can die right now and be out of his grace." "I know, you don't have to take it to the extremes Sandra." He paused for a second, "God I pray that you forgive me for cussing out that Lady. I am sorry. And I pray that this will never, ever happen again. In this I ask of you, in the name of Jesus, Amen." He picked his head up with a new glow on his face, the kind of glow as Moses had when he came down from Mount Sinai. The Israelites were afraid, but I know that it's just my daddy receiving the blessings from our big daddy in Heaven.   "See, how hard was that?" My mother smiled at him. "Wasn't hard at all; I just felt so ashamed about cussing that old lady out like that." My father carefully explained himself, using his words wisely in the process.   "I know baby, I know that the last couple of weeks have been extremely rough   for   you." "Tell me about it." My father threw his head down. "But you can't go around cussing family, friends, and old ladies. I love you Rodney, and I just don't want to see you hurt or out of favor with God. Go warm up the Jacuzzi, light some candles and I'll be there in a minute. As for you my sweet Precious, don't   follow   in   your   brother's   footsteps. That boy has the intelligence of an astronaut if he applies himself. You have that same amount of intelligence and passion for education as well. Don't let your brother talk you out of your education. Have a good night; see you tomorrow, and we'll   talk.   Love   you   baby!" "I love you too mother." Sometimes my mom does take things to the extreme. May God bless her heart.

"Hey, what was mama them talking about?" Justin pushed for answers.   "Daddy done cuss   this   old   lady   out." "What?" Justin looked at me as if he seen a ghost, maybe   the   Holy   Ghost   to   be   frank.

"Yes, he's been having some hard times lately." I looked over at Justin to see what would be his response.

"Still the same old Precious," Justin smiled at me wickedly, maybe he did see a ghost, or one of them demons that Pastor Hall was casting out a couple of weeks ago. "Why you say that?" What the heck is he trying to say? "You know what I mean Precious?" He gave me that same wicked looking smile. If I need to perform in exorcism on this boy, then lawd you gone have to teach me now. "What explain it to me Justin?" He's getting on my nerves. "You still love to take up for pops, no matter how wrong he is." He nodded his head in disappointment. Let me catch my breath before I say something stupid to my big brother. "Listen Justin, I am truly not condoning my father's actions. What he did to that old lady was truly wrong, but he's still just a man like you are. I can tell you still have some forgiveness issues to work out with daddy. The sooner you can forgive him, the sooner your life would take faith in the awesome power that God gives." "I know, I know, but daddy doesn't seem to do right." He smirked. "Justin, daddy's been trying to do right for the last five years; you just ain't been man enough to give him a chance." "Precious, are you that in love with daddy till you don't see how fake he could be? I believe he's putting on this big front. I believe he's still cheating on mama and covering it up." "Now why would you say such a thing Justin, huh? Why would you say such a thing? I'm going to bed." "Precious I'm sorry." "Don't apologize to me; apologize to your daddy. He's the one you've been hurting all this time."

JOSEPH

"Remember Joseph my step brother?" "Yeah, I remember Joseph, the boy that your daddy had out of wedlock with that hamburger lady." Maxine giggled. "He's coming down for the weekend," I openly hinted, not really looking for a response from Maxine.

"He's coming down?" Maxine shouted over the phone. "Yep," Why does she care? "He's so cute, girl. Hook me up with your brother." "Girl, no, Justin is not like that. The boy is the mere image of purity and righteousness." "You talk as if the boy is Jesus." Maxine whispered through the phone. "Well, he's not Jesus, but he sure seems to be on that path towards his divine appointment." "Girl, what are you talking about? The Joseph I met two years ago was funny, playful, and above all, very cute." "I believe that Jesus has a since of humor as well. Look at some of his parables, and don't you think he was cute? I mean, he is the son of God." "Don't start preaching to me now Precious." Maxine quickly took offense.　　　"I'm not trying to preach, I'm just saying that some of the same characteristics we have, God has. We were created in his image. God doesn't want us as Christians to run around like a bunch of stiffs. He wants us to love upon one another."　　　　"Oh, so when can I love upon some Joseph?" Maxine giggled hysterically. Now I know her mind done went to　　　　the　　　　left. "Girl you need to quit." I tried to show some restraint, but that didn't seem to work. The laughter in my voice was hard to contain, Maxine is a natural born fool.　　　"Quitting is not an option when I find the man I want."　　　　"Is that so?"　　I　slowly　questioned　her. "Yep,"　Maxine　assured　me. "Well Maxine, don't try to push yourself so hard on my stepbrother that it becomes a turn off." I'm feeling a little bit uncomfortable about her liking Joseph.　　　"Girl, I am a pro at it. I'm going to love on your stepbrother so clean, he wouldn't imagine that I like him; unless, unless you tell." "I'm not saying anything!" At least I will try not to.　　　　　　"But if I see you trying to do some freaky stuff to Joseph, then it's on, my friend."

"How could my little bit of darkness destroy his light?"　　　　The sound of her irritation pierced　　through　　the　　phone. "The same way Delilah convinced Sampson to cut off his hair."　　　　"Yeah, but I'm no

Delilah, and he's no Sampson," she's really aggravated with me now. "Maybe you're right, maybe I'm taking this whole thing out of proportion," "Finally, girl, you admitted what I was saying for the past hour. Look here, everything is going to be cool. It's not like I never seen a fine looking brotha before." "Speaking of fine looking brotha, didn't you like my brother Justin at one point?" This girl is no good. I wouldn't be surprised if Maxine had a crush on my daddy too. "Girl I never liked your brother Justin like that before. You need to stop trying me with that mess. I just had a small crush on him for like a few weeks." This girl is definitely out of her mind. What am I going to do with her? "Okay, Maxine, whatever you say. Hey, I've got to get off the phone, company's coming over." "Is he there yet," She asked softly through the receiver. "No stupid, I told you he's coming this weekend. Some of my mama's friends are coming by. Hey, I have to go, bye." Sometimes Joseph can be a little weird. I hope he is alright when he comes down to the great city of Orlando. Of course, I said that sarcastically. Seems like everyone around this city works for the Mouse. If it wasn't for the Mouse, I believe this town would be like any old washed up town in Florida. Joseph is pretty handsome. My father obviously has good genes because I am the meaning of beauty. Here comes all the gossipers, one by one as they enter our home.

"Hello, Precious," one of my nosey neighbors greeted me.   "Hello, Mrs. Margaret."   I   responded   nonchalantly. "How are things going for you these days young lady?"   "Well, you know, they are going alright. I can't wait to graduate from high   school   and   go   to   college." "Enjoy your high school days while you can, my love; because you will surely miss them when they're gone. I sure wish I could go back to high school." She looked up at the ceiling, re-hashing her   high   school   memories   as   well. I'm sure her old butt doesn't want to go back to high school. I don't understand how my mother could allow all these people in the house. Here comes Mr. Stan, he is Margaret's husband. Those two   are   total   opposites. "Hey Mr. Stan," I politely squeezed in another word.   "Hello Precious, you look well today; how is your brother Justin doing up in Atlanta?" I totally wished he didn't ask that question, but I guess I kind of had it coming.   "Well Justin is in his room, I can go get him for you. I'm sure he can tell you   all   about   his   college   experience." "No need to bother him, tell him I said Hi." Oh, so all of a sudden he doesn't want to know about Justin because Justin is actually home. Adults are such phonies. I pray I don't be like half of the adults I see when I grow up. Here comes my mother.   "Welcome, welcome everyone to our home. As you know I am the assistant coordinator for out area to help get out the vote to elect George Whip for U.S. Senator. I must say, it is going to be a tough month and a half coming up. So I'm definitely going to need your help with this. As you all know George is a Democrat and a native of Orlando. So this, this right here is the ground floor of his campaign. This is sort of my first time in the political arena. But I'm sure that I'll make a great assistant coordinator with your help. The coordinator of this campaign could not here today. But she does wish all of you the best of luck with the campaign. Now, before I start moving into the heavy stuff, I would like for all of you to meet my family. First up is my lovely husband Mr. Rodney Lewis. He's the one who will be keeping me balanced and out of the crazy house. Next is my beautiful daughter Precious; she's definitely my right hand girl. Also I would like to introduce you to my son Justin. Precious, where's Justin?" "He's probably in the back room playing video games." "Would you care to get him please?" I am so ready to be gone from this dump. These people are too stuck up. Let me go get Justin before my mom wets her pants. "Justin, Justin our mother wants you to come out and meet these snobby folks." "Yeah, sis, what's up?" He looks at me with his eyes bulging out of the frame. "Mom and dad are out front waiting on us!" "Dang! I was just in the middle of playing on the Wii." "We got to go meet Mama new friends. Pause the game, boy, and let's go." "Alright, let me." Before he could even finish his sentence, mother was yelling for us in the background. "And this is my handsome son, Justin. Justin, please say hello to theses beautiful folks." I don't know about beautiful; but if that's how my mother feels then what the heck. "Hello, what's, what's going on here mother." My brother asked. "I'm glad you asked. These people are here to get Mr. George Whip elected into the state senate. I am the assistant co-ordinator for this area. It's going to be a lot of hard work son; but with God all things are possible. Now back to our meeting. You two, Justin and Precious can have a seat. Thank you." "Okay, everyone, do you all know the platform that George Whip stands by?" I definitely don't know; he's probably a snake like the rest of them. "If you don't know his platform," my mother continued. "Then this is what his five basic beliefs are. Number one, he believes in freedom of expression. Number two he wants better health care for seniors in the state of Florida. Number three, he believes the death penalty should be removed all together. Number four, he wants to put in place better programs for teens on drugs and teens thinking about abortion.

And the fifth subject matter on his platform is a program he's created with his non-profit organization called Work the Drop. Do any of you know anything about his Work the Drop program, the idea that exists with it is purely for each student who drops out of high school? His organization finds a job for that student. Ten percent of that child's pay check goes back to Work the Drop. And what he does with that ten percent is put back five percent towards that child's college education. And the other five percent goes towards their G.E.D program. In its five year existence the program has had a ninety-five percent success rate. The students take classes at their leisure and many have already earned their bachelors from college. Right now, as you know, it's just in the Orlando area; but he would like to take it statewide. How many of you believe he can do it? "I do, I do, and I do." Everyone said in the room. "Well I wish they had something like this for college students," my mother hinted at the need for Justin to be apart of such a program. I know that was directed towards Justin, as he walked out the meeting. "So ladies and gentlemen, we will have another meeting in two weeks to give assignments and to see who's really serious about this thing. Otherwise we have refreshments in the kitchen. Enjoy yourselves. Go George Whip for state senate!" I can't wait till all of this is over. I wonder where Justin went. I guess its things like that which makes mama out to be beautifully ugly!

"Joseph my dear, welcome back to Orlando. How was the ride down from Tallahassee?" "It was okay, Sandra." I knew that my stepbrother looked good, but not that good. I see what Maxine is talking about. Lord please forgive me. "Well, I'm happy you made down here safe and sound." Yeah right, my mother does not like Joseph. She told me that every time she sees him he reminds her of daddy cheating with Ms. Hamburger. "Make yourself at home. I'm sure the rest of the gang will be happy to see you. Your father will be home in an hour. Precious is in the kitchen baking brownies and Justin is in the back room playing video games. Justin will also be working with his father this upcoming Monday." "Thank you for your kindness Mother Lewis." Thank you for your kindness Mother Lewis; he acts as if he's pleased with my mother. "Precious, Joseph is here." She yelled out with a slightly agitated demeanor. "I know mother, I heard you two talking." Duhh... "Well, how are the brownies coming along?" she looked me up and down as I walked in the living room to share my greetings. "They should be done in about ten minutes. Hey what's up Joseph?" This time I had an opportunity to look at his entire frame, not just that little peek from the kitchen, boy has he grown up. With a clean cut, heavily shaded eyebrows and a stature near daddy's six feet frame, this boy could definitely be model material. That brotha Tyson Beckford will have to come out of retirement once he sees the competition.   "Hello, Precious. I bring you and Sandra greetings from our father God in heaven." My mother examined Joseph for a few seconds and said, "Oh yeah, what did   He   say?" "He said, 'be blessed in doing well, and be not weary in good doing also.' Today is the day that the Lord has made and we shall rejoice and be glad in it."   "We appreciate you sharing that with us Joseph. I'm sure your dad would love to see that he created a little preacher." "Sandra, I must say that I am surely no preacher and definitely not worthy of the calling. I am just a mere servant of God." How humble is he, isn't that amazing? I love this boy; I wish Justin was more like him.   "Well, I'm going to tidy up before your father gets home. Maybe we can all go out to eat. In the meantime, you can go back there and play video games with Justin. Precious, the brownies should be done by now. And when you're done, I would like to speak to   you   in   my   room." "Okay." What the heck does she need to speak to me in her room about? I didn't do anything wrong. Joseph went to the back to play with Justin; while I'm busy here cutting up the brownies. My father should be here any minute now. "Yes, mother, what do you want?" I can't stand her sometimes, especially when it comes down to how she treats my brother Joseph. So what if he was a child of adultery. He didn't cause daddy to cheat with Gloria Hamburger. I bet, I just bet she wants to gossip about him. "I want to know why you have been staring down your stepbrother like that." Ooops, I got caught, but it's not like that. I mean he is my brother. "Like what?" I questioned her. "You know what I'm talking about Precious; don't play with me." "I'm not playing with you." I lied to her. "I'm going to ask you one more time young lady; what's up with you lusting after your stepbrother. You know that's incest." "Incest, Ma? First of all, I was not lusting after my stepbrother, and secondly, I was just admiring how handsome he is." "See, how hard was it to tell the truth? I will be watching you, young lady. I know your hormones are flaring and attitude increasing. So I got my eyes on you like a Hawk." Whatever, Ma!" She had me upset. I'm ready to flip out on her accusations. "Don't whatever me, young lady; go to your room. Wait till your dad gets home. We will discuss this problem tonight. And it will be resolved quick, fast, and in a hurry. And don't try to give me that innocent look, because you are not innocent."

"Rodney, your daughter has a crush on your son,

and I don't know what to do." "What wait a minute, what's going on?" Now she has my dad all frantic and all. He's looking around bull mad and disgusted.   "I said our daughter Precious has a crush on your son Joseph."   "No way," my father backed up.   "Yes way," my mother yelled back at him. Here come the stares at me.   "But, Precious, is this true?" My father held his hands close to his face, ready to wipe the excess sweat from his eye brows. Joseph favors daddy more, while Justin favors mama more. I don't know which one I favor the most; I guess it's probably a tie between the two. "Of course it's not true; you know how mother be making up stuff on me. I'm tired of this." "Hey, that's no way to talk to your mother; you hear me, young lady?"   "Yes, Daddy." Thankfully I didn't get his back hand. "Okay, cool.   Let's get Joseph in here." My mother interrupted and pleaded, "No, he has nothing to do with this. It's about our daughter having a crush on him, and I won't stand for those two being home together by themselves." "Okay, so what do you want me to do, Sandra?" He calmed down a bit, not wanting to waste precious energy   on   anger. "I want you to put Joseph in a hotel somewhere. Just keep him far away from Precious." "But I thought you just said he has nothing to do with this, Sandra. Please be clear about what

you're   saying."
Tell her dad, she is definitely taking this whole thing out of proportion.   My mom took a deep glance at me and began speaking. "So, so you want to put Precious in a hotel, Rodney?"   "No, I don't want anyone in a hotel, Sandra! Joseph will only be here for a few days. And like you said earlier, we will just make sure those two aren't here together by themselves!" My father's eyes flared up with anger again, confused by my mother's demands. "Okay, Rodney, I respect that. But I must tell you, if our daughter is pregnant, it'll be your entire fault." My mother deceitfully said. She's crazy; what rock of crack was she smoking? Lord God, please forgive me. But Lord my mother drives me crazy.   My dad picked his head up to speak, "Sandra, baby, you talking crazy now. Let's go to bed, baby; it's been a long day." "I had plans for us to go out to eat, and Precious even made brownies for everybody." My mother tried   to   redeem   herself. "I lost my appetite; I'm going to sleep." I can tell daddy was upset because he doesn't turn down food   often. "But, but Rodney." My mother pleaded once more. "No, I said no, Sandra! I'm going to bed, good night."   "Okay, good night. Come on, Precious, let's eat the brownies. Oh, call the boys to the kitchen." I looked at her and rolled my eyes.   "Justin

and Joseph, the brownies are ready." I stepped a foot away from the kitchen and called out their names. "Okay, we will be there in about five minutes." Justin said. My mother obviously heard what he said. She turned her head quickly and yelled out for them to come out the room instantly. Joseph just about did the hula-hoop as he pounced out the door. There is still no sign of Justin giving up his game. Mother hurriedly walked to his room and said, "Boy, I know you heard me, Justin; your brother Joseph is out the room at the table. But look at you Mr. College drop out. You are here playing the Wii. But you know what son; we got a problem, a big problem! I don't care if you're twenty-five or forty-two, you will listen and re-spect me in my home."

"Ma, ma, I just was playing a game. No need to get all excited about it. Dang, where's dad when you need him?"

"What did you say?" Her frustration boiled over. "You heard me. I said where's dad when you need him?" Justin answered back with an attitude just as bold as my mother had. "Your father is in the room sleep. Since when did you care about your father?" "Since you've been acting off the chain recently." Justin is so lame, people don't say off the chain no more. Did he already lose his sense of coolness by being here for a few days? My mom paused; she took a deep breath, and then decided to speak again. "Okay, Justin, here's the deal. There are brownies waiting for you at the table. You can care to join us if you like. If not, then you can do whatever. I'm tired of running around here barking but no one listening." Well that just makes me happy. The best dogs are the quiet dogs in my opinion. "Okay, Ma, thanks, bye." "Precious, let's go eat. Your brother is as stubborn as your father." I wonder why? "Anyways, Joseph is at the table waiting for us to come eat." My mother's eyes widened when she saw that he fixed all of our plates. Joseph is such a sweetheart. He truly deserves him a good woman. "So, Joseph, how are things going for you," my mother announced across the table. "Everything is going well," Joseph responded with such a charm. She asked Joseph another question. "So how are your grades Joseph?' "All A's ma'am." "What do you think about politics Joseph?" My mother kept drilling him with questions. "I think that politics are from the devil." Wow, that's pretty funny; and he said it so calmly. My mother's eyebrows lifted up so high, you would've thought she was having a stroke. "Okay, Joseph, so why do you think politics are from the devil?" Joseph looked up and responded to my mother by saying, "Well I believe it's from the devil because politics are filled with liars and liars can't make it to the Kingdom of

Heaven. Even the ones who claim to push for the most good are telling a lie. You see stepmother; there is a cause and effect to everything. And whereas one cause may be good to one group of people, that same cause may be poisonous to others.   "Okay, Joseph, you have a point. So, what do you think about Santa Claus? You know Christmas is right around the corner. I know you usually like to come here to spend Christmas time with us." My mother placed a stumbling block in front of him.   "I think that Christmas time is of the devil." If you thought my mother was having a stroke before, boy does she look like she's having a heart attack now. "And I'll explain why. Christmas has become so commercialized and about people receiving gifts. And if certain people don't get certain gifts, certain people get mad. Only Satan is about destroying   families,   not   God."
"One last question, Joseph, what do you think about having a girlfriend?"   "I believe it's from the devil. My belief is that we were never meant to casually date, but to immediately say our vows in marriage. Dating can cause all kinds of things I don't want to say. But I know one thing, God is good, but dating is not.

          "Girl, when am I going to see your step-brother?"   "He's here now, Maxine. I think my father is throwing a barbecue, so you're invited to come." I told Maxine with a little jealousy in my heart. I don't need Maxine turning out my stepbrother. "Precious, I will be there, honey! I will be there to lick the barbecue off your Brother Joseph's fingers."

Maxine is so nasty. "Okay, Maxine, you need to call on God and ask Him what your problem is." "Child, I got a thing. Me and God are like big homies. I will pray that He put Joseph right in my lap. Holla!" She would want him in her lap, just like a video vixen. "Alright, Maxine, don't bring that ghetto 'tude to the barbecue at the house. You will get kicked out of an already outside event." "Child, please, like I told you before Precious, I got me. I know how to play the role and make the boys drool." Exactly what I don't want her doing. "Bye girl," I rushed her off the phone, couldn't take another second of her sexual undertones. "Bye." Maxine picked up on my anxiety with her.

At the barbecue all was going well until Maxine showed up, I knew I shouldn't have invited her butt. "Come here Joseph; let me rock your world." Maxine said with a cunning smile. "Maxine, the only thing I'm going to be rocking is the word of God cradled in my arms." Maxine replied quickly with a comment, "But you know that you want me, big daddy." "Maxine, I do give kind thought to your persistency, but I receive no pleasure in the way you are speaking." He frowned, saddened with our generation's selection of woman, wishing that he'd find that diamond in the rough in marriage. A woman that's pure, never been touched by a man, this is the woman that he would want, and this is the kind of woman that he deserves, since he has pledged   allegiance   to   his   purity. "Yeah, pleasure, that's exactly what I'm talking about, Joseph." She licked her lips, ready to go in for   the   kill. "You are missing the point, Maxine; you are only taking out words that you want to hear, which quite frankly has nothing to do with what I'm saying. So, let me take it down a notch for you. I, Joseph Hamburger, do not want any kind of physical or social relationship with you. I'm sorry, but I'm putting my heart and soul into God. And I prefer to   only   lust   after   Heaven." She just couldn't take 'no' for answer. "Oh, Joseph, you are being so modest. It's okay if you like me and do not wish to share this with anyone else." Joseph yells out at the bottom of his lungs, "Precious! Precious! Please come and get your friend Maxine." Of course I stopped whatever I was doing with daddy and went right over to get Maxine off of Joseph. The girl was trying to turn a force of light   into   a   soul   of   darkness. "Hey Precious, may I speak to you in private please?" Joseph mentioned with a swollen face and   heart. "Sure, what's up?" We padded our feet over to the gazebo; no one was present there for the moment. "Why did you invite your friend Maxine to the barbecue?" That's a good question.   "Look, Joseph, the girl has been asking about you since I told her you were coming. She asked me about you the other day, and I told her that we were having   this   barbecue." "Okay, it's cool, Precious. I just don't want her sweating me as if I'm some deep sea bait." "Well, Joseph, you are kind of like some deep sea bait. A guy like you is hard to find. When my brother was your age, he had already lost his virginity. I don't know exactly when, but what I do know is that you are a hard catch. And women like Maxine will throw themselves at you like a good bible study.   You know how when you have a good bible study you can't seem to get enough of that preaching. You just want more, and more. Well, that's how women will be over you my brother. Speaking of brother,   where   is   Justin?" "He's probably in his room playing video games." Playing video games? We are having a family barbecue, what is he doing playing video games. That boy is losing it.   "Can you tell him to come on outside." Hope I wasn't being too bossy with my request.

"Yeah,   I'll   go   tell   him." "And I'll go handle your new girlfriend." "Precious," he finally lent a warm smile; this was the Joseph I knew.   "Okay, okay, I'll see you in a few." God ain't ever made an ugly man, and Joseph is definitely far from ugly. He is so humble, till it makes you want to just give him an award for it. I think that my friend Maxine was taking things overboard. My stepbrother had clearly stated that he didn't want anything to do with her; yet she still was trying to manipulate him into being with her. I guess she'd make a good saleswoman.   I don't know what I should say to Maxine about Joseph. I did invite her to the barbecue. I don't want to embarrass her, but I also don't want to lead her on with Joseph.   "Listen, Maxine, I know you are my friend and all, but Joseph is fed up with the way you've been pressuring him into dating. I told you once before, he doesn't do   this   type   of   stuff." "What does he do? Sit around the table and read the bible all day. Come on, Precious, don't trip. He is just like you and I. I know his type. Although, I think he's cute. I'm not into wasting my time on guys who don't want to spend some of their time with   me.   So   thanks,   Precious,   bye." Maxine gave me quite a bit of information to absorb. I wasn't quite ready for that. "Wait--- Maxine. I'm sorry for saying it that harsh like I did, but I'm only trying to look out for my step-bro." "So what, are you his Guardian Angel now?" Maxine caught an attitude with me.   "No, but I am his sister, and if my brother wants to stay a virgin till he's married, then that's perfectly okay with me. I just, I just don't want anyone to try and

take   advantage   of   him."
"Well, okay, Precious, good night. I understand
exactly what you are saying. And what you are
saying is a bunch of bull crap."   The degree of
her words scorched the center of my heart, this
was   bruising,   and   this   hurts.
"No, Maxine that's not what I mean. Being a virgin
myself, I understand how hard it is to try and con-
vince your mind to stay away from the evils of
this world."   "Evil? Who are you calling
evil?" She doesn't get it.   "I'm
not calling you evil, Maxine, I was just defining
evil towards the deeds the flesh craves to do. Believe me, my body has gone through some
changes, and I've gone through more than enough
temptations. Yet my God has delivered me."
"Listen, Precious, I'm not a hit it and quit it type of
girl. I do want to have a decent and honest relationship with a guy; then we can kind of hit it
later. "   "But what about the cost
Maxine?   What   about   the   cost?"
She puffed up, noticing the smoke bellowing from
the grill, we both began to salivate, picturing the
smooth tender cuts of pork slathered over homemade sauce. This was a prescription for good eating, that's right, just what the doctor ordered.
"What cost; I don't charge my man to get any of
this sweet loving. What do you think I am a prostitute?" Okay that was funny, but clearly not what
I meant.   "When I say cost, Maxine, I'm
talking about the cost of your faith. I'm talking

about the cost of contracting a disease or even worse, getting a free first class ticket to hell."
"Yeah, I hear what you're saying. But I'm young; I got a long life to live. I'll get my life right in a few years."
"Sonya was young too; look at what happened with her life." She paused for a second, speechless and frustrated; she looked a way, till finally she regained her senses.   "That girl committed suicide; I ain't trying to kill myself." I can't believe that Precious would think that low of me.
"You know what, Maxine, that's cool. God will truly work on your heart on his time. I can't force you to believe or think one way or another."
"Good, I'm glad you woke up and realized that, Precious. As I told you before, I'm good; me and God got our own thing going. We on channel two, while you on channel four. You understand what I'm saying."   "Yeah.
I guess." Weird moment number one. "It's not just something that I realize, Maxine; it's something that I understand your heart needs. You see my friend we are all beautiful people, but it's our sins that makes us ugly.

MY HOUSE, MY RULES

"Honey, honey." Yes, Sandra, what do you want?" My father growled, content with what he was burdened with. Apparently he was too busy to answer her the first time. "Baby, it's been a week now, and Joseph's mother hasn't come to pick him up. The boy has been in school for a week and I'm kind of worried about this whole thing. You know how I feel about him and Precious being alone." "Listen, Sandra, for the last time, those two are brother and sister. There is absolutely nothing going on between them besides brotherly and sisterly love. Who you should be worried about is our son Justin. He can't seem to keep his mouth shut around the girls that work in the office with us. The boy is going to have a baby in no time at the rate he's going. I just don't want him to make the same mistakes that I made." "And he won't my love, he won't. Joseph and Precious are brother and sister, but not like Precious and Justin." "Listen, baby, like I told you before, if it makes you happy, I'll put Joseph in a hotel." His anger was a little more subtle this time, versus the last time the two of them had that conversation. Seems like all the family quarrels happen over the kitchen table.   "No, that's okay. We just have to keep a close watch on those two."   "Okay, whatever you say Sandra." He's had enough. "Well, what's that supposed to mean, Rodney?" My mother glanced into the very frame of my father's soul, seeking an answer his mouth wouldn't give. She wanted to know what his soul was saying; she wanted to find that bond that glued them together, even during times such as this.   Over-whelmed by what she saw through the eyes of the love of her life, she looked away. The passion, the promise and the hurt ran deep through the very core of his cuticles, she saw apart of him that she had forgotten about. She saw the love of a father's passion for his kids, and with this type of passion, she knew that he would do anything to protect them   at   all   cost. The burden she bared is tough, reminiscing on the ten years that she was a single mother raising Justin and I. She was all too familiar with the nights she cried and cried for daddy, heart broken by the adultery he committed. I can remember when Justin use to run to her room night after night to be her comforter. She had to be the rock of the family then,   but   things   have   changed   now.

"It means that I can't believe you are bringing this up. They haven't done anything wrong or immoral their whole lives. So why do you expect them to now?"   "Because I too was young once, and at an age of pure confusion because my menstrual cycle and different things were just ticking all over the place."

        "Sandra baby, you still tick all over the place." He brightened up a bit.   "Wow, that deserves a laugh." Finally a sigh of relief. I'm sick and tired of them talking about Joseph and I getting it on. Not only was it sick because of incest, but also it's just unimaginable to sleep with my own brother, no matter what side of the family he's on. He's still my brother; my little brother at that.   My dad began to speak, "Sandra baby, I know that it's been rough lately, and we've been arguing about the kids, worrying about the election, and struggling in this economy. You know what; let's go out on a date tonight. Just you and me; we'll have Chinese and catch a movie. How does that sound?" "It sounds good, Rodney, except for the fact that I'm incredibly behind on grading papers and I promised to help Precious with her homework." "Baby, I'll help Precious with her homework if she needs help. And for the grading papers part, why don't you have Justin to help you out; he was a college kid. So are you down for dinner and a movie?" "Yeah, I guess." She replied with a tender smile, happy that the two could come to agreement.

"Well, let's get ready to go. You know how I feel about eating late." His ears rang high and the moment was ripe, he did well to step up to the plate and squash the quarreling. My daddy is always the hero, he's my Superman. "Yeah, if you eat too late it'll give you gas for the whole night. Believe me I know. I'll head to the shower; would you like to join me?" She moved her blouse to the left a little bit, giving him just a few seconds to see her wide high hips. Just like a young whippier snapper he said," Sure, my love, make sure the bubbles are ready." Now that's sweet, they sure know how to kiss and make up. Hope they don't make me another brother or sister soon. It's already enough drama with Justin and me; and now Joseph.

"So, Rodney, what's on your mind baby?" "I don't know Sandra, the kids, work, and I just feel a little stressed out. The thought of Joseph and Precious doing adult activities is enough to make me scream. I guess I just don't get it. Why do you feel so passionate about that stuff? They're just brother and sister for Christ sake." "Rodney, I'm sorry for taking this whole thing overboard. I just know how kids are ever growing, ever smelling themselves at that age. I just wanted to make sure they don't smell each other too much." "I accept your apology Sandra, and I'm sorry for getting upset with you. I love you Sandra, I love you with all my heart. You are like the rose which stood still in a crowd of thorns. You are my lover, my heart, you are my everything."

"Wow Rodney, that's so sweet. I don't know what to say. The Chinese food is good; maybe that came out wrong. I mean your words that you spoke cast pearls upon my heart. Were you practicing that in the mirror?" "No, baby, I just made that one up all for you." "Rodney." Sandra dipped her eyes a bit. "Yes." He wiped the residue of sour chicken and noodles from his beard. "I've been thinking, baby." She dipped her fork into her noodles, swirling them around like a tornado, making sure to cover her fork, while catching the drip of the bourbon sauce smothered through her plate. "Yeah, what have you been thinking about Sandra?" He tensed up a bit, even straightening himself in the chair. "I've been thinking about how remarrying you was the best decision I could have made in my life. You have really been strong and took a hold of this family." She blushed, eyes wide open and ready for round two with the man of her life. "Sandra, honey, it is my duty to be the responsible man in taking care of this family. I was born to protect not only our seed, but the woman who bore those two for nine months. You are my heavenly answer and my unbridled gift, you are the joy of my life, baby." "But Rodney, we're getting older, and Justin still seems a little held back from you."

"Honey, that's okay. Although we get old, our love still grows strong. Besides, you know black people don't look their age anyways. As far as Justin is concerned, I truly believe the boy will come around. You should see him and I at work, we make a great team you know. On his lunch breaks he makes sure to come in and talk to me. I feel that he's really been opening up more, a lot more than I expected. Yes, he still does have some instances of hesitation, but I can tell the boy loves me. I know he trust me. I just have to let him be the man I taught   him   to   be.
"Wow! That's great Rodney; I didn't know that you two were communicating like that." "Yes we are, Sandra, and I believe that it will only get better."   "Wow, look at the time; its ten minutes till the movie starts. Remember, we also have that George Whip meeting at our home tomorrow, so we can't stay out too late."   "Yes, I remember; let's go baby." They paid their tab and tip, and then ran off like two teenagers falling in love for the first time.

        "So   mother,   how   was   the movie?"   "It was so funny; it had me rolling out of my seat." She looked awfully happy today. I haven't seen her happy in a while. Maybe mom and dad should go out on more dates. It's always good to get away from this house from time to time. Although she didn't help me with my homework, that's cool though, Justin helped me with my homework while Joseph was in the back room listening to the bible on iPod." "How did dad like the movie?" My mother still had a grin painted on her face, she's looked so cute. "Your father enjoyed it as well; he just about fell asleep twice. But when he was up, he laughed his tail off. We had an overall good time. We should do that more often. Sorry I didn't help you with your homework last night." "That's okay, mother, Justin helped me out with my homework. I always like to see you and daddy happy. I think I may have made an 'A' on my paper." "You really think so?" She blushed like a school girl. "Yes, I think so." At least I hope so, wouldn't want to disappoint. If I don't make an 'A', then it's Justin's fault. "Precious, I'm going to need your help. We have the volunteers coming over for a meeting with the George Whip party. I need you to help me here in the kitchen, and I'll get your brother Joseph to tidy up a little bit. Your dad and Justin should be here any minute now. But I assume the guest will start to show in about thirty to forty five minutes. Joseph! Joseph, come to the kitchen please darling." I hope he hears her. "Okay, I'll be there in a moment stepmother." He makes his way to the living room with us. "Joseph, I need you to help tidy up the house a bit. We have company coming over and Precious and I have to fix something in the kitchen right quick. Are you ok with that?" "Yes, I love to serve, however I can be of assistance

I'm happy. I'm just so happy to spend time with you guys." My mother interrupts and says, "We are happy you are here too. Okay, enough of the chit chats. The guests will be here in about twenty minutes. Justin and your father should be here in five or ten minutes." "Okay, I'll move as fast as I can." Joseph understood with a wide smile. He's so handsome, you can't help but to love him. If Maxine had her way she'd devour him like a roaring lion. I hope that Maxine gets it together before it's too late.

"Welcome everyone, welcome back to the Lewis residence. Have a seat, make yourself feel comfortable, and please enjoy yourself. Before we get started, I just wanted to point out some of the house rules." Here she goes with her rules. "Rule number one, there is to be absolutely no smoking in our house, no walking around the house without an escort such as myself, my husband or one of our kids. The third rule is please do not go in the refrigerator. Precious would have a heart attack if she seen someone taking her juice out of the refrigerator."

"Hey, Sandra, why so many rules?" One of the guest looked around to see if anyone else disapproved of Sandra's rules, to his surprise, not a soul stood up or gave a hint of disapproval. "Glad you asked. First off it's my house, my rules. Secondly it's to keep the wear and tear on this house down significantly. Thirdly, if you don't follow the rules, then the campaign meetings will be held somewhere else; immediately." "No need to push, sister, I was just asking!" He sat back down, humiliated by her reprimand and disapproving of her perceived lack of respect for him. "Hey, my fault. I'm sorry Mr. Whip, just been under a lot of pressure lately." She eased her tone a bit, recognizing the stir she just created in front of the very man she is rallying to elect. Mr. Whip took along deep pause and said, "Tell me about it, feels like this campaign is going to take the life out of me." I hope it takes the wrinkles out of him too. He already looks lifeless. Finally, daddy and Justin have arrived home. My mother retained her composure, after one good sip of Chardonnay, how ironic is that, "Alright, everyone, we are going to start the meeting here. I am so blessed and humbled to be in the presence of future state senator Mr. George Whip. Everyone give a round of applause!" Everyone applauded with cheer. "Thank you, thank you, Sandra. It is a pleasure to be here in your home, even with all the rules. To all of you who have started here on the ground floor with me, thank you too. It gives me so much pleasure to see all of you here to support and work with me. It is with your hard work and dedication that I believe we will be elected. Now you may wonder why I say we. I said we because each one of you represent the faces of this great state of Florida." I hope he doesn't give a long stomp speech. "Florida residents are known for their hard work, hospitality, and of course diversity in culture. You all are the shining light of what the sunshine state represents, and a beacon of hope to millions who call this state their home. So without further due, I just want to say thank you. Thank you, thank you for helping me as we go door to door, pillar and post letting everyone know who I 'am, and what we are all about. Go---Florida!" The volunteers erupted with cheer, chanting his name, shaking hands and pledging their support of this man. I'm happy he's done talking, seemed like he was spitting after every word he spoke. My mother strides back to the front to control the crowd. I hope she excuses everyone out of the house. I am tired and ready to go to bed. Lord, please help me to be a better girl, a better person and above all a better example of your love. Lord, I know I haven't done my best to be all that I can be, but I pray that I'd be better than anything I've tried to be,   amen.

"Alright, ladies and gentlemen Mr. George Whip has said all he needed to say. We thank him so much for showing up. We appreciate his wisdom and thank God for such a man as this. All has been said; my husband will now come up and bless us with the grace for the food. And we can all relax and enjoy each other's company; come up Rodney."

There goes my daddy; I love my daddy. He is the greatest.   "Dear father we thank you for this food we are about to receive, let it be nourishment to our bodies, in the name of Jesus Christ I pray, Amen."   "Wash your hands everybody, wash your hands."   My mother loudly declared.   She's such a mother, crazy and funny at the same time. I can't believe she got into it with George Whip. She laid down the rules and laid down the law at the same time. Joseph looks so sad in the back; I wonder what's wrong with him? I can't recall ever seeing him so depressed. I pray he's okay. Good night God! I'm going to bed.

GEORGE WHIP

"That Sandra Lewis is a feisty one. What was she doing running the meeting, in the first place?" George was not pleased; the evidence of his displeasure was stroked by the lines through his flushed face. "Well, Mr. Whip, the director called in sick." His assistant happily answered his question. "Who does that Lewis lady think she is; disrespecting me in front of those people? Does she know who I am? I'm George Whip; I'm King Tut of politics in the State Of Florida. No one disrespects George Whip and gets away with it." "But, sir, you did ask her about the rules. I'm sure she just wasn't having a good day. She did apologize to you as well, sir." His assistant tried to make the best out of the situation. "That's not good enough. I'm going to make her pay." His fist met the desk in a match of pure maple wood and compact bone, the maple wood won that match while George let out a big growl. "Ouch, these bastard tables will put a hurting on someone. I want you to get rid of this table and have the movers here by noon tomorrow."

"Ok sir, but what are you going to do to Sandra, fire her? She's a volunteer. And she's one of your biggest supporters. I think you may be taking this Sandra thing a little overboard George." He squinted, a little shaken up about his bosses comments, knowing that George is a man of his word. "Hey, talk to me like that again, and your job will be overboard along with the rest of the cronies that work for me." "Sir, I'm only making a reasonable suggestion." "Keep your suggestions to a minimum. I'm not in the mood for listening to what people want. I already know what the people want. They want me. And those volunteers are lazy under her assisted direction. I can't find a better group of screw-up's on this side of town. Fine me some Mexicans, they will be sure to get the job done." "Yep, politics as usual, my friend. Politics as usual." He shook his head, not knowing which way to go with George's last statement. "Hey, take this note down for me as well. Please make a reference to the media to stop sticking me next to those retarded kids during a photo op. I am sick; I am sick and tired of them slobbering all over my Italian suits. I know they are retarded, but you'd think they'd have some mode of self discipline while taking a picture." He leaned into his desk, still bothered by the bruise he received a few minutes prior. "I'll make a note of that. But I also must warn you that retarded kids and babies give you the most points in

the polls."   "I
don't care about the points in the polls. I care
about my thousand dollar suits. Polls don't mean
a thing to me. You hear that, polls don't mean a
thing. The only pole I care about is the one down
the street with the ladies doing their thing for a
dollar. I tell you, they ought to vote for me. I've
given the ladies enough dollars at that club for
them to start a franchise. Can I just find some foster kids who are normal minded and call it a day?"
He loosened his tie and checked the blogosphere.
"Hey, what's with this kudoblog, the girl has
bashed every program I have started. She is trying,
not trying, but she is defacing my name, and can
you get Scooter to pay her off. I'm tired of these
bloggers popping up like cockroaches trying to
mess up my good fortunes. I use to think that reporters were slimy, oh no, these bloggers don't
have a blood vessel running through their heart."
He sighed, pausing only for a moment's breath.
"These bloggers are heartless and I want to get rid
of her because she has too many followers. Just
yesterday she had one-hundred thousand hits. Is
Scooter on the line yet? Tell him he has a budget of
two-hundred and fifty thousand dollars with this
girl, if the money doesn't work, tell him to call
Skip to revert to alternative methods. Got that,
who does she think she is? I'm like an Angel of
light. At least that's what my master tells me, only
he comes to kill, steal and destroy. Well, maybe he
and I are one in the same. "   "I'll get on the

line with Scooter right away sir." He dialed Scooter, and then reflected back on their conversation concerning the foster kids. "Sir, I haven't met a normal minded foster kid, they all have some sort of mental instability. A lot of it comes from depression and a lack of love shown to these kids. Foster kids will work. Not only will it bring great attention to the problems happening in the foster homes, but it will also be excellent PR for you too sir." George paused, he thought about everything his assistant dished out, curious as in how using foster kids will be good for his over all campaign image, "Now that just may a problem. I can't have the focus slanted off of me for some throw away kids! I need all the attention focused on me, and me alone! Do you really want to win this election?" "Yes, of course, sir, I do." He dropped his pen in fear; the clinging of the clipboard was heard thereafter.

"Well, you need to act like it, my man." George lightened his tone a bit, but his physical features said   different.

"With no disrespect, Mr. Whip, you did suggest foster kids." He picked up his clipboard, pen and paper with sophistication, happy that his boss slouched back in the chair.

"I know what I suggested; I just don't need the attention straying from me. I am the star of this show, not a bunch of abandoned kids that no one cares about in the first place. I'll just take pictures with the Mexicans that we have, case closed." "Mr. Whip, I don't think that would be a good idea either." His assistant nervously clicked his pen. "And exactly why is that?" He moved forward in his black leather business class seat, this time less than four inches from the nostrils of his assistant. Backing up a bit, his assistant took to caution, "Taking pictures with a bunch of Mexicans would only bring up immigration issues. You definitely don't need an immigration issue in this state. Besides, the Cubans who make up the majority of Latinos in Florida don't always get along with Mexicans. Taking pictures with a bunch of Mexicans will not only hurt you, but it could possibly cost you the election all together."   "Are you serious?" His hands flung up to the ceiling, forcing his seat to move back into its intended position, he slammed down his laptop and spewed a couple of mo-fros and bittersweets. His tongue was ripe with anger and oily with defeat, he had to find away to give his campaign a better lift this election cycle.   "I'm as serious as the vanilla in vanilla ice cream, Mr. Whip." He responded with his head ducked down and eyes slightly bent into his chest for safety. "Who can I take a picture with? Who can I take a picture with that doesn't take attention away from me, and doesn't offend people at the same time? Find me a good local pastor, one who is clean, has no past history, and the people just love him."   "Mr. Whip, that wouldn't be a good idea either."   "Jesus Christ man, can you be positive for once. I'm going to call you the bad news blues, and then I'm going to fire you! You remind me of that prophet who kept giving bad news to the King. The king had to shut him up."   "Jesus Christ indeed, sir, that king eventually was killed because he did not heed the words of the prophet. The only problem with doing a photo op with a pastor is the subtle reality that it connects your campaign to a particular religion. Let's be honest here sir, you're not a religious man, and there are no clean cut pastors. I'm sure if you dig deep into their histories, you will find all kind of dirt on those pastors. Look at what they did with Jeremiah Wright and President Obama. They practically slaughtered President Obama in the media for his affiliation with Jeremiah Wright. I've heard a pastor say that all have sinned and fallen short of the glory of God. We simply can't use a sinner to help catapult this election. Like that pastor said, all of them have sinned. "Tell me about it. I give up; I give up. This great state's sunshine has totally turned my campaign to darkness. What happened to grace and mercy?" "Well, Mr. Whip, you can always take a picture with you and your wife. The media loves to see husbands with their wives. You two make a beautiful couple."   "What are you talking about; you have never seen my wife." He was offended.   "Oh, well I just assumed you two would make a beautiful photograph." "Do me a favor; let me do the assuming and you just do the thinking. Got that? Besides, my wife and I won't make a good photo either. I cheated on her too many times and she's ready to get a divorce. If the press gets a hold of her wanting a divorce, they would be eating me up for take-out. Get it, they would literally take me out of the election if news spread that my wife and I were divorcing, it would be worst than that John Edwards fellow." Disappointment continued to show through George Whips face.   George continued, "So we both agreed to have an open marriage until the elections are over. She comes home just like she normally does and I basically give her an allowance to help her keep quiet about this. Of course we sleep in separate bedrooms and the kids don't really notice it. I'll be better off taking a picture with my next door neighbor's wife than   with   mine." "I wouldn't be so sure about that either George, I mean you are getting divorced for messing with other   people's   wives." "Of course you idiot, I know that, I was sleeping with my next door neighbor's wife. You need to get out more, catch some fresh air. Is this office wearing on you?   "   "How about taking a picture with you and your mother, George? How about a picture with you and your mother? These pictures   are   usually   drama   free." "She's dead!" He said with an expressionless composure, a sign of just how the day had been going for him. No way to explain the pity in politics. "Well, I'm sorry to hear that, how about your father?" His assistant tried to smooth it out a bit, but to no avail. "He's retarded. He's out there in the nursing home and doesn't even know my name. I hate seeing him like that." His face fell, couldn't stand another thought of his father's mental and physical decline. He'd rather keep the good memories of his father, the memories of his father as a workhorse, a true man's man. His father worked the graveyard shift for the Ford Motor Company for twenty-five years before he was promoted to a senior level position. Although his father was satisfied with the wages at the time, he'd often come home to an aching back and swollen feet from brutal nights work on the assembly line. This was also during an era when companies compensated their employees well, gave families such as the Whips a place to stay and a pension plan to rely on, his father always said, 'that was the good ole' days.' His words are more like that of an infant now. With the onset of Alzheimer's, he has lost all the memory of his youth. His life at the senior center is now the life that one would come to expect from an eighty-two year old sheltered with snow-white whiskers and frail limbs. But yet if one were to truly live a full life and make it through the circle of life, then, just then would the world see that the picture of death is just a common place for all mankind to start a new beginning. "I insist sir; a picture with your dad makes good press Mr. Whip." He toggled his glasses a bit, making sure he could see without blemish George's response.   "No, I told you! No pictures with retards!" George was unmoved and rattled a bit, the pain of a lost mother and father was as lethal and venomous as an Indian Cobra.   "But he's your father," his assistant said with an unadulterated compassion for not just his boss, but maybe   even   his   friend. "No, that's not my father. I lost my father seven years ago. That's about the time he entered that place. That was just about the time my mother died of breast cancer. The man went crazy and was never the same. I can't stand going to see him like that. I usually see him twice a year." "Okay, well, do you have some brothers, sisters, or cousins we can get a good compelling picture with?" He gripped his notepad, hoping that this would be the Holy Grail of pictures since all other attempts failed.   "My brother and sister do not like me. My brother is a pastor up in North Dakota and he says that I'm the son of the Devil. I wouldn't whole heartedly disagree with my brother's statement, for Satan is my master, the Prince of Darkness. At the end of the day, he is who I serve, and none other will come before him.   My sister started hating me after I refused to see my father once a week. She lives in Atlanta with her husband and two kids. And the only cousin I know and grew up with was a foster kid. Believe me, it's a long story and I don't have the time or the energy to talk about my family history. "Okay, well, it sounds as if we are quite out of options here Mr. Whip." "Tell me about it, it's the story of my life; always out of options." He released a much needed breather for an otherwise stressful day. "Okay, I got something." The assistant said cheerfully. "How about taking a picture with the kids from your Work the Drop program?" "That's a negative." His head swayed east and west in despair. "If I receive anymore suggestions, I'd probably shoot myself, and then bury my carcass in the grave while dialing 911. You got me going nuts man!" "Come on Mr. Whip, you started such a helpful program and now you don't want to take a perfect picture with the kids you've helped." "First of all, my friend, it won't be a perfect picture. I've been kind of fudging the numbers a little bit."

"What do you mean?" He shook his head with despair. "What I mean is that the state requires my program to have a ninety-five percent success rate in order for it to receive state funding. We are not at ninety-five percent like we claim. We are more at the eighty-two percentile." "Wow, but that's still a good ratio for kids who had no hope in the first place." "Yes I know, but the state doesn't see it that way. All they care about are numbers, not lives. I can't take a picture with these kids because I don't need any inside investigations into my program that could destroy me and its very existence. I can go to jail for giving false numbers, you know. I'd rather handle this when I'm in office again. Then I will have the opportunity to change the rules while in the senate. Besides I have a lot of buddies I need to do favors for as well when I get up there in office. They wouldn't mind if I change a few rules to help myself out, as long as I'm helping them out as well. My master already has people in high places; I'm just the fallen piece to the puzzle." "That's outstanding boss, you know how to capture the people's heart, and once you capture the people's heart, you'll eventually win their soul." "That's just what I was thinking; you are a very smart being, Zagan." "Well, you do know that I am good at deceit. This comes without question about my character; it's your character that troubles me George." "I'm ok, I'm ready for this, even evil has its share of good," he declared. "Perhaps, but the best know trick is to be wise as a serpent and clever as a dove. It's not what you do that makes a difference; it's what you say you will do that means all the difference. Give the people a little hope, and they'll run to you like cheese in a mousetrap, give them a greater hope, then their caught. What has to be done requires precious time and you winning this election." Zagan leaned back in his chair. He complemented himself with his all black silky choir like attire, an outfit he has cherished for eternity.   "I believe that the perfect political picture would be a picture of myself. I'm going to have a great smile, a great suit, and shake hands in the process." "Are you sure this is what you want to do?" Zagan's eyebrows lit up, tipping deep into his skull. "Yes, I'm sure." He said with a sly grin. "Well, you can't go wrong with taking a picture with yourself. I must admit, Mr. Whip, that could be viewed as a sign of pride and politics as usual, not a sign of humility."   "I do have pride and I am a politician! What else do you want from me? I bet you'd like nothing more than for me to take a picture with a pizza delivery boy, wouldn't you?" He   quickly   took   offense. "Yes, I would like that. But that's not the picture you need right now. You need a picture that represents your character, your strength, and your destiny to help the people. For it is the people whom will elect you, so being in photos with people will only promote you as a person of the people. And people like people who seem to like people. All you have to do over the next few months, Mr. Whip, is like people and they will love you. Pick up some babies to kiss, and hug some pregnant women. Although I would caution you on the latter part, seeing as your record with woman is below average. But now is truly the time, sir, to get your PR engine rolling. And the only way to start that clock is to be around people; good people that is.   The people's perception of you has to be flawless. You are a beacon of hope, and a shining light for the works of our master. If you can rule the state, you can rule the nation, if you can rule the nation, you can rule the world. This land belongs to us, it is our sweet inheritance, and souls will know the true god of this world."

SPECIAL GUEST

"Come on, Precious, we're going to be late. Rodney, what are we going to do with our daughter, honey?" I hate when they talk about me like that. "I don't know, baby, she takes after you." I am nothing like her. I don't know why we have to go this breast cancer awareness dinner anyway. I would rather stay home and do my homework. Justin looked mad and my brother Joseph was just being Joseph. That's just Mr. Cool, Calm, and Collective. "Precious, you have two minutes to get in this vehicle. I don't have time for the attitude." Why is she getting on my nerves? Sometimes I just hate her guts. I know I shouldn't hate her guts as a Christian, but she just tries me too much. "Finally, you are ready young lady, I'm proud of you." She tried to ease the tension, but my pent up frustrations with her were going no where. I guess fake it till I make it will just have to do for tonight. "Precious, are you okay?" My daddy noticed my detached composure. He definitely knows me. "I'm okay daddy, I'm okay." My daddy is such a sweet heart. "Justin and Joseph, are you two okay back there?"

"Yes." The both of them answered in unison; although Justin clearly didn't sound okay. Off to the breast cancer dinner, as daddy said a prayer before we hit the road. The event was like twenty minutes away. I had a feeling that it was going to be a long night. Maybe some good things would come out of this dinner, like finding out some of the signs of breast cancer and a how to prevent it. Otherwise, where's my iPod?

"Ladies and gentlemen, welcome to our annual breast cancer fundraising dinner. All of you who have come from all walks of life, we greatly appreciate you for being here to support these women that you see on this panel and many more throughout the state who are living with breast cancer." The audience applauded. The speaker continued, "Their use to be a point in time when breast cancer was a taboo subject, now women across the state and country are benefiting from the knowledge and pre-screening they receive because of your dollars which help out countless numbers of women and men get the attention they deserve. Many of these women could not afford the screening and medicines on their own." I wish this event was over by now; I'm struggling to pay attention to this goofy looking light-skinned lady with her church hat on looking like one of the characters in Tyler Perry's plays. She continued to burn our ears up with rhetorical chatter, "Many of you all have heard their stories and witnessed their struggles, pain, and triumphs over breast cancer." She did speak compassion, long-winded, but compassionate, as she rattled through the pages on the podium. "Listen I tell you, breast cancer can be beat. Many, many women can avoid death if they simply do their annual checkups, and immediately report any abnormality when they see it." She paused to transition to the next speaker, she obviously lost one-fifth of the crowd because of her lengthy speech. There were two ladies right behind me chit-chatting away.   "So without further due, I will introduce our next guest who does not need any introduction. Our next guest is running for state senate and proudly supports us, and we endorse him. Ladies and gentlemen, please give a warm welcome to Mr. George Whip." The crowd roared as if a rock star was about to take stage and play his greatest hits. So that's why we're really here, to see that Whip guy speak. I thought we heard enough of him at the house. This breast cancer thing was pretty cool, until he showed up on the stage. Something about him I just don't seem to like. Maybe it's his smile, the way he talked to my mother, or just the fact that he's a politician. I don't know; let me hear his speech, maybe his speech will let me know what he's really about.   George walked slowly to the stage not giving a care in the world about other people's time, as long as he was seen on the bright light and big stage, I guess that's' all that really mattered to him. "Good evening, good evening, it gives me great joy and pleasure to speak with all of you today. Seven years ago I had my own personal encounter with breast cancer." Really, I thought that men didn't get breast cancer. Wait a minute, men do not have breast, do they? "Yes my mother fought a good fight with breast cancer and she finally succumbed to it. If my mother would have known what many of you know now, there is about a ninety-nine percent chance that she'd be alive today." I knew men didn't have breast, what am I thinking. He politely paused to give a brief silence for the memory of his mother. "So when my secretary told me a few day s ago that the president of this organization invited me to speak, I not only felt a sense of reassuring, but an opportunity to speak as a man about a woman's problem. Not to say that men cannot contract breast cancer, but the majority of new cases are found in women. My mother use to always tell me to stand up and be strong for another. I am so sorry that I couldn't stand and be strong for her during her last days. But I am proud to be able to stand up and be strong for you now. " He continued, "Every single day women across the world are being cured of breast cancer. Sadly enough every single day a new mom, sister, or aunt is being diagnosed with breast cancer as well. These are the women we are looking for." He has a point; one of my aunts was just diagnosed with breast cancer. George continued with his speech, but he had all of the crowds attention, "These people and more are the reasons that great organizations such as this exist. They exist because we love our families. They exist because they love us. We exist because God gave us a privilege to live. Living is a not a right my friends, it's a privilege. It's a precious privilege based upon the principles and knowledge that there is something somewhere that's greater than us." The crowd was silent, everyone was thinking about their family members who were affected by not only breast cancer, but cancer of any kind. "I am George Whip, and I am running for your Florida State Senate. Thank you everyone for having me here tonight. It is both a privilege and a pleasure. God bless you and the great State of Florida, good night!" The crowd broke their silence and roared with cheer for Mr. Whip once more. His speech had me absolutely speechless. Here I was thinking that this man was just here to look for votes. But he really knows what it feels like to have a family member who had succumb to breast cancer. He has my vote. Lord, please forgive me for judging this man before; I should have never judged him. For all I know, he could be a Mighty Man of God. "What did everyone think of George's speech?" My mother questioned us on the ride back home. "I feel like I'm about to puke, I thought his speech

sucked!" Justin said out of spite, signaling the conclusion of his displeasure from the moment we
left the house. What's gotten into him?
My mother replied, "That's not nice, Justin, we all
have to support Mr. Whip." "You asked my
opinion, ma. I just don't like the guy. Hey, I'm not
the one who brought the politician to the family."
My mother did a quick one hundred and eighty degree turn in her seat. She looked Justin straight in
the eye and said, "What's that supposed to mean?"
"I just don't like him, ma, I don't want to argue
about it." He settled his chin below his neck, a sign
of defeat and or a request for peace.
"I thought he was great!" I quickly put a chill to
the tempers that's been seeping through the car
seats.

"Well, I'm happy to know that someone was
happy with his speech. What did you think about
it, Joseph?" Oh boy, why did she ask Joseph. Politics is definitely not his thing, my mother should
know better than that by now.
Joseph continued to look out the big bulky windows of our SUV like a deer in the headlights. Does
he even know what day it is?
"Joseph," My mother would not back down.
"Yes, oh, I feel that he had a great speech, it was or-
chestrated very well. He definitely makes a great
orator. I just don't feel right in my spirit about
George Whip the man. George Whip the speech
maker is okay. George Whip the man, I think there
is something else about him which just does not

align with my spirit.   "Rodney, will you please say a prayer over our family and Mr. Whip. Pray especially that we are making the right decisions not only for our family but for others."   "Okay my love, I'll pray. I'll pray for it all." My father responded sarcastically, as we were only about five minutes from home. After Joseph made his comment, everyone in the car was silenced. What if Joseph is right? What if there is something else about George Whip; maybe a darker side I suppose.

FELIPÉ

"Felipé, when are you going to get some rest, señor?" "When Mr. Whip decides to pay me more, Mama. I struggle on the farm day and night. I do it for you Martina. I do it for you, you and the kids." "Felipé, I love you, señor. I love your heart, your desires, and your dreams. But I miss you. At this rate, my friend, you'll be dead before you're fifty. You're doing at least sixteen hours of work a day, how much is Mr. Whip paying you now?" "He was kind enough to increase our wages by one American dime, so I'm earning three dollars an hour now." "Felipé, that sucks. I make more in an hour at Wal-Mart." She rumbled through their bedroom dresser to look for her pay stubs, just to make sure she was correct with her analysis. "Martina, we've already gone through this, baby, I have no education. This work in the field is the best wages I earn. It beats working in Mexico for quarters an hour." "But Felipé, my taco, I miss you. I miss being able to rub you down. I miss seeing your eyes. You're always dirty when you get home. You are always so tired, señor, you don't even jump in the shower like you use too." Her plea couldn't have come soon enough, as he exerted the smell of a hard day's labor. Martina picked up on every strange scent that attached itself to Felipe; from the highly concentrated stench of manure to fertilize the land, to the dry blood of chickens on his boots.   This was an average day for   the   Hernandez   family. Quickly taking to offense, Felipé decided to rebel," Martina, I don't have time for this Americanized conversation. My father and my father's father worked and worked the land. The women cleaned up and fed us. I don't ask much of you Martina, but I do ask that you love me, respect me, and say nice things.   The dirt on my body represents the work on the land, the scratches on my face represents the tears of this man. The scars on my shoulders represent the weight of this world, and the marks on my back represents   the   past   behind   me." He closed his eyes a second; thinking about how hard his father worked the Great Plains in Texas, his father was a first generation immigrant to arrive in the U.S. All his father wanted was to live the dream, the 'American Dream' that is. A dream that was not as pretty once he crossed the border, but he had faith. He had a faith unknown to those that were born in the U.S., his faith taught him how to survive and care for his six kids. Felipé will always remember his father as the man who laid down his back for him, so that Felipé could pave a better

way   for   his   son.
"Martina, I'm tired of it all, just like you. I--I just
don't know what to do." His eyes could not with-
stand the pressure anymore, the tears made their
way up through his pupils like an underground
water source looking for an exit strategy. He
pulled the hem of his wife's garment and prayed silently for a miracle.   "Well
why don't you just sale drugs," Martina suggested
nonchalantly, totally eclipsing the mood.
"What?" He looked at her with grave disbelief.
"Just kidding my taco, don't be so serious Felipé.
What happened to accepting a joke señor? The
drug money is good though." She gave her two
cents, plus a quarter for good luck.
"Martina, I've had enough of you for one night. I
love you, but, I want to get some rest." The despair
and displeasure in his voice could be heard
through the cracks and crevices of his children's
bedrooms.
For it is the plight of the father to bear the burdens
of his children. When all else fails, he must do
what he has to do in order for his children to survive. Just like a bird would go thousands of miles
to feed its chicks, so is the spirit and fortitude of a
man to travel even further for a better future. His
father had already traveled the distance, now it
was time for Felipé to carry the torch.
"Well you better give your kids a kiss back there,
they have been asking about you all week."
"What do you mean Martina? I've been here all

week," he said, with his face flushed red. There was nothing like the wrath of a father when his kids were involved. Even the wrath of God was kindled for the sake of his people, the Israelites, during the time of Moses. Martina tapped her finger nails on the kitchen table out of frustration, "But they haven't seen you Felipé, they don't see you. You're gone when they go to school, and they are usually asleep when you get home." Felipe' could not argue with the truth, he knew that the long hours he labored had kept him from one of the most precious commodities in life, his family. "I have to do better, Martina; I have to do better." He stretched his lips forward to kiss his wife, but unbeknownst to her, she kept right on with the conversation. "With little to no education, papa, it's hard. It's so hard, my taco." "Martina, why do you call me that, I told you I don't like that nick name, I believe that it is degrading to our culture and heritage. Calling me my taco reminds me of the commercials that, that American company had playing across the screen with a Chi Wawa dancing and talking." " Felipé, I've been calling you that since we were teen lovers. Remember when I told you how much I love tacos because they have such a great hard shell and soft and warm on the inside. Well, that's always been you Felipé, hard on the outside with a soft spot for people on the inside. You have always been my protector, my best friend, my lover, my taco."

"Ok Martina, if you say so. It just sounds a little strange, but if that's how you feel about me, then I guess we can just keep that nick name between the both of us."   "Okay." She cheered on his response. Deep within her being, she was happy to know her husband can still be romantic.   "Martina," he called for her attention. "We raise our children to be better than us. They will have nice jobs, the finer things in life, and they will truly be able to live the American dream. I sincerely thank Jesus Christ for all he has done for us, but there are so many times I feel that I am living in America with just the dream."   "Felipé, it's okay, we will survive. I love you so much, my taco. I just want you to be home more to see our kids as they grow. In five years our daughter will have her Quinceañera, and our son is only six now, and he's already starting to ask about girls." "Wow, my little princess will be fifteen in five years. Please don't remind me; they grow up too fast." He shook his head in silence, still baffled at the thought of his children being grown and on their own. He could remember the time when he was just a teen, chasing after woman and helping his father on the land. Before he could put a hand on any woman, he knew to ask the girls' father for permission first.   Felipé often realized that it was best to get to know the brother of the girl he wanted to date, because the brother was usually the one that put in the good word with the father, once that bond was in place, the sky was the limit. He and Martina met at the Fiesta Drive-In Theater in Carlsbad, New Mexico on June 18, 1993 to see the block buster smash, Jurassic Park. Martina was fifteen at the time of their date, and it was the first time she was allowed out with a guy without parental supervision, Felipé was sixteen and borrowed a car from one of his older cousins. That night for the two of them was more than re-markable; it was magical, as they both were ner-vous wrecks, not wanting to get the other in trouble with their parents. It wasn't Felipé first date without supervision, but he preferred to put his best foot forward. They were so into each other, barely noticing the dinosaurs roaming the earth again on the screen, at that very moment it would take a meteorite to break them apart, and the two have been as one since that magical night at the Drive-In movies. "You better go in there, and give them a kiss, I'm sure they'll be happy to see you." Martina snapped her husband out of his spell. "Where is mother?" Felipé asked with grave con-cern. "Your mother is sound asleep in her room Felipé." She comforted him and dispelled any negative notions he may have had. "You don't want to wake her up. You know how much of a grouch she is when she's awake."

They each shared a laugh, a much needed gesture to lighten the atmosphere. Felipé glanced on at Martina, he discovered that spark again, that magical spark from their first date at the movies. It was because of this spark that has held them together for nineteen years. "Papa, you're home?" His son ran to him like a sprinter in a track meet, Felipé was barely through the bedroom door. "Yes son, I'm home. I love you." His eyes were at it again, creating tiny mud circles on his face, he could not contain himself, Felipé love for his children is just a little lower than the love that God has for all that are His. "Papa will you read me a story?" He smiled, displaying each of his young pearly whites, the same color as the milk that keeps them strong and healthy. "Sure my son, I will read the both of you a story. What do you think about that my little princess?" He cuffed the arms of his daughter who was only partially awake, but nevertheless awake just enough to give her daddy a peck on the cheek, and share a smile. He was overwhelmed by her small perky lips and cheek bones that sparkled like Martina; he silently thanked God for blessing him with two beautiful and healthy children. He called them his two little motivators, each time he sees them, they motivate him to do better and want more for himself, which would ultimately be more for them. It was moments like these, which he knew would only last for a short window of time. The moment a father and his kids can still share in the beauty of their innocence. "Ok kids, I'm going to share with you all a story about Fernando Hernandez the Great." The kids chuckled at the title of the book. "Shh...time for the story." He pulled up a chair and sat in between his son and daughter's bed. His son laid flat on his back with batman pajamas on reeling in anticipation, while his daughter used her pillow to prop herself up a bit to stay awake, pondering if she had heard this particular story before. Felipé began, "Once upon a blue moon there was a little boy born in a small village in Mexico. The little boy was born with little arms, little legs and a little head. All through out his life and in school, the kids would call the little boy names. They bullied him, they teased him, and the people of the village began to worry about his life. So on one fateful afternoon, the village leader decided to have a race. The race was to see who was the fastest in the village. The village leader had a good idea who was the fastest because he always saw the little boy get away from the other Chico's that teased him. And the little boy would run fast and fast away. So the village leader made a declaration, he said that whoever wins the competition would be crowned leader of the village. Whoever lost the race would also be under subjection of the village leader. The boys that often bullied the little boy were both fast and wise; they looked at a chance at leadership as a way to get rid of the little boy that was different from them. The bullies teased the little boy all before the race, telling him he would never win the chance at leadership, they said he would never be anything more than a midget." Felipé was interrupted by his curious son, "Papa, what's a midget?" He smiled.

"A midget was the little boy, they are people that are just a bit smaller than you and I, but they are people like anyone else." "Ok daddy, you can finish," confidant that he understood his father a little better, but because he never encountered a midget before in life, it was hard for him to conceptualize people being shorter than himself. Felipé continued, feeling a sudden swing of tiredness, he skipped a few parts of the story and maneuvered to the end," The boy who was different was actually the boy who ended up winning the race. Then he was crowned Fernando the Great. He was given the opportunity to get rid of the Chico's that bothered him, but instead he did something that the village would remember for centuries. He called the boys to his tent, he was surrounded by armed guards and the bullies were afraid. Fernando Hernandez the Great greeted each boy with a hug and declared for each of the bullies to have the best in the land. The village people were shocked; some were even outraged that Fernando Hernandez the Great could do such a thing. The former village leader's heart was broken because his intentions were for the exact opposite of the boys that bullied Fernando. The former leader wanted judgment for them. When asked why he did it, Fernando Hernandez the Great told his village citizens that he did it because the bullies had made him to be great." He paused for a breather, glancing into the weary eyes of both of his children, yet they hung onto his every word like a sponge. "You see kids, Fernando Hernandez the Great also said, if it wasn't for the bullies running after him every day he would have never won the competition. Every day that he ran, his legs grew stronger, his legs got larger, his arms got wider, and he also grew wiser." "Is that it papa? Is that the whole story?" His daughter wallowed out of her trance, still trying to figure out the familiarity with the story. "No, it's not my daughter. The moral to the story my children is this. Fernando Hernandez the Great wouldn't have ever been great without the obstacles the bullies placed before him. You see kids they gave him a challenge. They made him appreciate them, more than they hated him. So greatness my prince and princess comes from hard work and persistence. Every hardship can teach you both to be great. And greatness does not have to come with an iron fist; it can come with a simple hug and kiss. Goodnight." He tucked his children in and gave them a hug and kiss. Both of his children sighed, as they fell fast asleep. Felipé watched as their precious little stomachs rolled up and down with light breathing. "This is my future, this is my dream, and perhaps the American dream will be lived by them, May God Bless America and Mexico too."

GOD IS GOOD

"What is up with your mother Joseph? What? She doesn't want you anymore?" "No, stepmother that's not it at all. Truth be told, my mother believes that I am better off staying with you guys." My mother lowered her voice and said, "Well, you just about missed a couple of days in school in Tallahassee already Joseph. How are you going to make up for it, son?" "Wisdom comes from God; all the knowledge in the world can't prepare me for the knowledge that the Father has stored up with Him." Joseph looks so handsome with those pearly whites, and curly jet black hair. His smile was so intense, yet so passionate at the same time. "Well, I understand all of that Joseph, and I love the Lord too. So, let's bring this back down to earth. How are you going to make up for the classes you've missed? Hey, you see me, I'm a teacher, and I just about had a heart attack when I missed just one day of class." I don't know why my mother has to be so over the top with her emotions. She needs to quit. "I'm sorry if I may seem redundant in saying this, but like I said earlier, God will provide me with the necessary wisdom to complete and pass the classes." "Okay, whatever you say Joseph, I--- just need you in school somewhere. And that somewhere just might be Morning Glory High School." "Please don't send me there." Joseph uncharacteristically pleaded with my mother. "Why don't you want me to send you there and why are you scared?" "I'm not scared; I'm just disagreeing with going to that school?" He lowered his head just slightly lower than his sculptured broad shoulders. "Why?" My mother probed Joseph, licking her fingers on the chocolate cake batter. Finally, the last thing she has to cook for the night. Joseph mediated for a second, deciding to choose his words carefully, "I don't want to go to a school full of liars, fornicators, gossipers, and thieves; just to name a few." He picked his head back up, restoring his confidence and my mother's anger. "You have two choices Joseph and I hate to do this to you, but you must get back in school. You can either call your mother and have her pick you up from here, or you can attend Morning Glory High School while living under our roof." "Well there ought to be a Christian School around here somewhere stepmother. I just can't stand to be in the midst of such sin." He was scorned. My mother paused for a second, placed the chocolate cake in the oven, the continued, "Maybe your mother was able to afford to send you to a Christian school. But unfortunately Joseph, this family cannot afford to send you there. I love you as if you were my own, but I just can't do that. Look at Precious, she's still a virgin. Yes, she may want to date and do things, but you know Joseph? The bible says that we are all in this world, but it doesn't mean we have to be of the world. Keep that in mind my son.   You say that you are a Christian and a great man of God. Show the people at Morning Glory High School that you are that. Listen Joseph, you may just be the light that these kids need to turn their lives around. Believe me when Justin was in high school up in Tallahassee, all I wanted from him was to be a role model. But the real answer is he's not. He's not the role model type; he sort of took the opposite approach, but you have that true chance at being that piece of good the whole school needs. She patted down her face, making sure to dry up each wet molecule that seeped out of her pores. Moving from the oven, she pulls out the wooden chair which stood alone, waiting for her to sit next to Joseph. "As my grandfather use to say, it's hard to see a candle in a room full of light. You carry that light my son, let it shine where it belongs.   And I said, my son to you because it's about time I treat you as my son Joseph. You don't have to call me stepmother anymore; you can just call me Mama." Sandra wiped another wet molecule from her face, but this time it wasn't sweat, it was a tear. And just like that, her tears began to follow in line like ducks, one after the other. "For many of the years that you've been alive, I've held a grudge against you and your mother. I hated your mother and disliked you, all because of what Rodney did years ago. Joseph, I am sorry for the way I have been treating you. I am sorry for all the negative energy you have received from me. I judged you even before I knew you son. But right here, right now, I see an awesome man of God. I don't see a fifteen year old boy. I see an example of love, purity, and strength that exist in your heart that I wish I had." She grabs his left hand, as Joseph looked at her dumbfounded, maybe he is in the same state of shock as me, "Once more Joseph I apologize, I love you, and please forgive me. God is good son. God is good." Tears continued to roll down my mother's eyes like I've never seen before. Tears of freedom perhaps, maybe even tears of joy. Drop after drop rolling down her beautiful face, tearing apart the makeup both physically on her face and in her soul.

Joseph stands up, picks up my mother's hand, "I forgive you mother, now can I give you a hug?" She looked at him like a drone, still feeling the surreal nature of this moment; she did not know how to respond to his request. He looked on in silence waiting for her response. Her lips lifted, but words could not spew out of them. Then with a heavy breath and the extracting of deep bulges of snot, she obliged. The whole room burst into a symphony of weeping, just in time for my father to arrive. "What's going on in here? Sandra, what did you do to the boy?" My dad was blown away with the atmosphere he was witnessing in the kitchen. You would think that the T-Bone would be the main event. Not tonight. "What, what are you talking about Rodney?" My mother responded with a slight anger. Rodney did not get a chance to witness her and Joseph hug each other, which was probably the realest hug the two had ever shared. But I can also understand how daddy would take to offense considering how Mama had never really treated him with dignity over the years. "Joseph is crying Sandra, what did you say to him?" My father was upset for nothing. He demanded an answer. "What's wrong with him?" My mother refused to respond. I decided to intervene, "Daddy, nothing is wrong. Mama and Joseph are fine; they were just making up for old times. I think you and mom should discuss this alone. Daddy, you shouldn't talk to mom like that. She did nothing wrong." My father turned around and looked at me as if he had some hot grits on the stove and was prepared to use it. A look of confusion filled his handsome but angry face. His eyebrows arched up a bit and cheeks pressed into his skull. He couldn't say a word; he took off his shoes, put down his bag and sat down at the table with us. I think he realized his mistake; an overflow had filled the room. It was one of the first times I stood up for mom against him. I've always been in his corner first. Everyone just looked at each other.   I felt for my pulse to make sure I was still walking up-rightly, thank God, I'm not dead, and daddy spared us.   Jus-tin enters through the front door, he looks just as confused as daddy was looking, but he doesn't say a word. Justin tries to pass us all and heads to-wards his room.   "Hold it right there, Justin, come here and take a seat. This family has some talking to do."

THE RACE IS ON

Life is like a nightmare waiting to happen. First you think that you're not afraid of the dark, and then you find out that the dark is not afraid of you. My family had a big blow out the other night; I barely want to talk about it. The demons which corrupted this family years ago seemed to have reared their ugly faces the other night. I'm not one to start trouble, but I do believe that the family talk was one worth doing. Although we all disagreed at times, God still kept us victorious. Joseph is starting school with me as of tomorrow and my mother and father are on speaking terms again. At first I was afraid because I haven't seen those two mad at each other that furiously mad at each other since I was a kid. But I guess it was about time the truth came out about how my mother felt about Joseph, and how my father felt about my mother's feelings towards Joseph. Of course Joseph didn't want any part in it all, but he said a few things and stayed for the ride as well. My brother Justin felt the same way as Joseph. He didn't want any part of the mess, yet he also added in a few words. I was not happy at all about the way my father was speaking to my mother, but I guess in the heat of the moment, every-thing comes out wrong. Only time will tell how the relationships with each other have truly been mended.

"Fifteen days left people, fifteen days left. In fifteen days we will be electing one of Florida's next State Senators. That Senator ladies and gentlemen is Mr. George Whip. I don't care what they say about him in the polls, he will be elected. The fast talking Joe Weeks will not beat us in this campaign. Joe Weeks he can fast talk himself into the losers' column." My mother gave her stomp speech on stage at the local park in front of a crowd of about a thousand volunteers and sup-porters. My father cheered her on while seated be-hind her as George Whip approached the stage. "My fondest thanks to you Mrs. Lewis, you and your staff have done an excellent job with this campaign. I appreciate your enthusiasm and dedi-cation to such a noble cause as this. And what can be nobler ladies and gentlemen than the oppor-tunity to serve your fellow man. Sure call it polit-ics, I call it servant hood. How ever you would like to call it," He wipes his face. "However you would like to call the flow of knowledge in dedication for the greater good of its people, I call that an accom-plishment.   The race is on ladies and gentlemen. We have approximately fifteen days to get the word on every street as to why I should be elected. You all know my platform, many of you heard me speak before and some have seen the commercials. Yet I must tell you this ladies and gentlemen, none of this matters if in fifteen days my name does not come up as the victor. All the promises, all the hard work means nothing if victory is not achieved. So I ask all of you my fellow Floridians to go out and text message, email, and talk about me on your social networks. Let's post up some flyers around this town, let's knock on some more doors, and let's all be victorious this upcoming election. Thank you and God bless you." The crowd roared with anticipation and support, he waved at the crowd and blew a few kisses as he handed the microphone over to the director of this campaign; she has a few words to share.   And that was probably the tenth speech I've seen Mr. Whip give. With the exception of his Breast cancer speech, all of his speeches I've seen have been pretty general and there really aren't any issues he covers   that   can   relate   to   me. What about teenage rights? What about premarital sex? I know that he has that program for basically drop outs. But it's no program for me. When will he start talking about the issues of abortions? Morning Glory High School has some of the highest rates of teen pregnancies and teens who get abortions in the state. I don't know, maybe I'm just asking for too much. Maybe I just want adults to pay attention to our needs more and not just brush us off like a gnat hovering around their face. I'm a human being, I'm important, and I shouldn't have to be eighteen to have that ability to express those issues. I'm not asking to be different; I'm just asking to be heard.

"Mr. Whip, that Sandra woman is turning out to be a great additive to our campaign. Did you see her compassion and unblemished love for the well being of your campaign sir?" "Shut up, shut up!" Mr. Whip barked at his assistant. "I still don't like the lady. An embarrassment taken once is an embarrassment for a lifetime." "I do understand your opinion sir; I just really admire her passion for this campaign, that's all. You know, as of six this evening the television has Mr. Joe Weeks up by five points on us." "I don't want to hear a thing about Joe Weeks, he's a crack, a scoundrel, and he's weak." His face flushed red; something else seems to be bothering him besides his opponent. "You're right sir, I apologize. Can I prepare you a cup of coffee while we wait for the reporter to get here?"

Mr. Whip loosened his tie," No, coffee is not necessary. Coffee is for the weak. I am strong. Coffee preys on people senses, then nerves, and most importantly it distorts their level of energy. For many, coffee has a strong hold on people; they can't wake up without it. But I tell you this, my humble assistant, coffee has no bearing on me." His confidence was rejuvenated and skin tone restored to its natural state. "Mr. Whip, what type of ad should we place for these last two weeks of the election?"

"The type of ad that will destroy men's souls," referring to Joe Weeks. "I want to crush Joe Weeks where it hurts. We've been running all these phony baloney nice ads during our campaign. Now it's time to get down and dirty. He stated it. He went after my Mexican labor force. Now I'm going after his family. I need you to find whatever dirt you can find on that Joe Weeks guy; anything to hurt his character. I need names of prostitutes if he had any. If he didn't, find someone for him. I need records on his mother, records on his father's spending habits. I need voting history; I need a full arrest sheet on my desk tomorrow. I need anything, I say anything I can put my hands on to nail this guy to a cross. This rookie Weeks is no survivor; I'm the survivor. I know what it takes to run this state, and I need him to go down." George took a deep breath, and then continued on with his evil plans to destroy his candidate's good name. "Florida is traditionally a conservative state. If we nail this kind of dirt on Joe Weeks, he wouldn't have a decent chance to get on his knees to pray. As a matter of fact, he'd be on his knees begging for us to pull the plug on the ads. So get to it, get to it now. I need everything on my desk by tomorrow morning! Get out of here!" Mr. Whip waved his assistant out of the room as he waited by himself for the local reporter to show up.

"Thank you, Mr. Whip, it's a pleasure for

you to have me here today," the reporter said. "The pleasure is all mine, Melany." "As I stated before over the phone, I'm just going to ask you a few questions about your campaign. The questions will be brief as I know you have a busy two weeks ahead of you up and down the state."

"Take your time, Melany." Mr. Whip comforted her with a smile. "You don't mind if I call you George, do you?" They each shared a professional smile.

"I don't mind at all." He moved around in his seat, searching for the exact spot which makes him comfortable.

"Okay, let's get started. You say that your campaign is a campaign for the servants, how is that true?" She gave him the floor to speak. "Well I am ecstatic that you asked that question. You see, Melany, too many politicians go into politics hoping to be served. I'm running for senate as the servant. I don't expect anyone to run halfway across the town to serve me coffee. I get the coffee myself. I don't expect for my assistants to read entire bills of legislation without me reading. I believe that I have to be the one willing to serve before anyone else lifts up a finger. There's an old saying that goes a little bit like this Melany, it's called, Lead by example, and leading by--." Melany cuts off George to move onto the next question.

"Onto the next question George, how do

you honestly feel about Joe Weeks?" He shook his head," Do you want me to give my on record or off record opinion?" Melany chuckled a bit and replied by saying, "Just give your honest opinion Mr. Whip, and know that we are on record. "Well, Melany, I believe that Joe Weeks is a very fine young man. I believe that he harbors the ability to produce great results, and I even heard that he is a fine Christian man too." "Do you consider yourself to be a fine Christian man as well?" Melany gripped her pen and pad for the anticipated response. "Yes, I sure do. The good Lord God has blessed me with a beautiful family. I have a spectacular wife, beautiful children, and each day I rise I can't help but give the glory to God, and I--." Melany cuts off George again, before he could finish. "Onto the next question George, Is it true that you've been harboring illegal workers to work for you?" She looked up from her pad, while her eyes met his. "No, that is nonsense, I don't know of such things. My opponent has falsified that tad bit of information about me. Hey, I'm a true American, and I only hire Americans to work for me. I have nothing against the Mexicans, but Americans need jobs too." "Mr. Whip, your opponent has suggested that you are a strad- dle the fence kind of guy. Are you a straddle the fence kind of guy Mr. Whip?" George took offense to Melany's question and said,

"Melany, do I look like a straddle the fence type of guy?"   She rectified his anger and said, "I don't know George, you tell me?   He looked at her, dotted his eyes and said, "No, I'm not a straddler. I never have been a straddle the fence type of guy. Are we done with this interview Melany?" "Yes, we can be Mr. Whip. I had a few more questions, but if you feel uncomfortable, I'll take my notes and leave." She said with confidence and security.   He responded with anger, showing her his true colors, "Yeah, I think we're done. You aren't going to do anything but deface my name. You reporters aren't worth the paper you take those little notes on." Mr. Whip lashed out aggressively.   Melany paused for a second, and then went on to say, "Well I'm awfully sorry you feel that way about me and my fellow reporters Mr. Whip. It sounds to me like you have something which you are trying to hide. And you're right; a reporter can be your best friend or perhaps your worst enemy. I would have liked to have been your best friend. So once again I apologize, and good luck on your campaign." She smiled, working her back side as she headed for the door that   leads   out   of   the   office. "Oh, by the way, don't forget to check your morning paper." She opened the door and slammed it behind   her. "Good night, Melany." He said with a dismal look on his face. He looks like a freshly pierced pumpkin on Halloween. All the life force has been juiced out of him as he appears to be a hollow shell with a half smile. What a beautifully ugly person he is, his heart is never up to any good.

DECISION DAY

"Today is the day people, today is the day. Today we are going to leave all the trash talking behind us and focus in on this special day. A day which all of you will witness not just a moment in history, but a moment in liberty and justice for all. Up until this time, everyone has been rallying up the troops. All of you have been some of the best volunteers I could have ever asked for. And your work will surely not been in vain." "I, George Whip am more than ready this day to be your next Florida State Senator. Ladies and gentlemen we have roughly eight hours to influence the minds of our fellow Floridians to vote for me. So without further a due, let's get out and rock the vote. God bless Florida and God bless America." George Whip smiles as he waves at the crowd while walking off the stage. He is dressed in a pinstriped black suit, vest, and blue tie. "I thought I said no reporters." George Whip said to my mother as he looked on at Melany from the local newspaper. She is fast approaching him and my mother with her pen and paper on hand. "Mr. Whip, Mr. Whip may I speak to you for a second?" Melany looked at him and didn't crack a smile. "I thought that we were done with this a few weeks ago. You've had your chances to ask me all the questions you needed. Besides, today is decision day; there is nothing you can write on that paper that will change the hearts and minds of the people of this great state today anyway. If you will excuse me, I still have a little campaigning to do. Speak to Mrs. Lewis; she knows all about my campaign, I'm sure she'll be able to answer all your questions."

Melany looked around and said, "Well, would she be able to tell me about your daughter Mr. Whip?" "What daughter?" Mr. Whip asked as a vein peeked out of the side of his head. "Sonya Moten, you know the one who committed suicide a couple of months ago." My mother interrupted, "That's your daughter!" Melany briskly turned around and said, "Yes, that was his daughter." "Is this true Mr. Whip?" My mother questioned with shock and disappointment, hoping that the man she has rallied for in all these months would say something that made sense.

Sweat riddled his face, as the look of anxiety and confusion overwhelmed him. "George is this true?" My mother asked again. He walked off from behind the stage, greeted the crowd again and drove off with his assistant; never once turning around to look back at my

mom   or   Melany.
"You see, it's true, he has nothing to say, because
he's been covering this thing up the whole time.
Reports show that he didn't even show his face at
the funeral. From the police report that was filed,
it showed a note and that your daughter was
around her during her last days. Your daughter
and the note spoke of excessive abuse by the
father, but they never could figure out who the
father was since Mr. Whip told his family to go
under an alias for a last name which is actually his
middle name.   "Well how
did you find all this out, and how do you know
about my daughter?" My mother frantically
asked.
"Your name is Mrs. Sandra Lewis, correct?" Melany eyed her with caution and suspicion.
"Yes."
"Well, just to ease your frustrations you and your
daughter have nothing to worry about." A sigh of
relief developed for both Melany and my mother.
It's just that when Mr. Whip said your name I was
taken back a bit to know that you are working for
the same man which you all have filed a claim on."
"But I did not know that he was her father."
"I know, no one does, Mrs. Lewis. I am an investiga-
tive reporter with the paper, you can come closer
Precious."
"Hey lady, you talking to me," I asked, barely able
to hear anything over this noisy crowd. Everyone
is still rallying for this Mr. Whip, while my mother

and this reporter are in shock and awe. "Yes, I'm talking to you. Now both of you hear me out, Mr. Whip neither denied nor confirmed that Sonya Moten was his daughter. But the very fact that he walked away when I posed the question leads me to believe that she was his daughter. I have never seen his wife or children that he claims to have."   "Yes, you're right, "My mother responded, "He says to have a few children and a wife; but I never saw them   on   the   campaign   trail." "Well, it gets even better than that, I asked him a few weeks ago about harboring illegal workers to work for him, he said it was untrue. But I took the liberty to look at a few court cases that were against his business. Buried under the massive legal jargon, I found a case against his company re-lating   to   illegal   aliens   back   in   2002." This new news struck Sandra's nerves, over-whelmed by what she was hearing, she wished she could just run away.

Melaney continued inspite of the look on Sandra's face,"Not only is Mr. Whip harboring il-legal aliens, but he's also not paying his workers their fair share. There was a recent filing against Mr. Whip and his company for unfair pay; it was filed   by   a   Mr.   Felipe`   Hernandez." With a sudden outburst, "Oh my God, oh my God, who is this man? Listening to all of this reminds me of when my husband cheated on me years ago. I   had   no   idea   any   of   it   was   going   on."

"Mother, that was fifteen years ago."
"I know baby, I'm sorry. Just listening to this reporter lady put me back into that same place of not knowing who to trust. I'm so sorry, I shouldn't have mentioned it. So, Ms. Melany, why are you telling us all this stuff? What do you want us to do?" "Well Mrs. Lewis, quite frankly there is not much for us to do. I wish I would have gathered all this stuff a couple of weeks ago in my original reporting of Mr. Whip; but the facts were a little sketchy and he has a lot of pull everywhere." "All we could do now is get on the blogosphere, I can do a late report which will be posted on our online edition of the paper, and I can try to see if I could get on television with this."

"Have you interviewed his wife yet?" Sandra asked frantically. "No." Melany exhaled, "I'm going to see if I can get her on TV. Her testimony will at least give a level of authenticity to this story. What I'm going to need you to do Mrs. Lewis is round up the troops and tell them who the real George Whip is." "No, I mean I don't know if I can do that." She hesitated. "As painful as it is, and all that he's done, I don't have that kind of power to do that."
"Look at you, look at you Sandra, you just don't get it. You have all the power; Mr. Whip trusted you with a very powerful position in his campaign. Now if he did not trust you, you would have been fired a long time ago. Do you hear me?

Don't come telling me about power, that's the problem. We women let men like Mr. Whip run and terrorize this country to hell, while we sit back on the sidelines scared, passive and defenseless." Whatever happened to women's rights Mrs. Lewis, whatever happened to bridging the gaps of employment with equal pay and equal rights to promotions for all men and women? Many white males are afforded these luxuries on a daily basis while the weak and the minorities have to continue to fight for equal pay. Sandra my love, you may not have been physically abused, but there are countless women each day that are being abused, raped, and taken for granted because we woman who do have power, choose not to exercise this power by making a difference. What we want to try to do over the next six hours of this campaign is to force Mr. Whip to step down and wipe his name off the ballet. We want to flood the phone lines with angry people calling in and complaining; asking for his removal from the ballet." Sandra cross examined Melany and asked, "So, what's in it for you?" With a look of shear disappointment, Melany said, "To see that dirt bags like Mr. Whip never get to see another day in the Florida State Senate; that's what in it for me." She said somberly.

"So, are you going to help me or what, time is not on our side?" Melaney picked back up the pace.

"I'll help you; Precious go tell your daddy that I'll

be home late tonight. Also tell your brothers to help you clean up the house." "Clean up the house? For what? "Okay mother, I'll do it, see you later."

"This is the Channel Nine News live here in Orlando. We have just one hour left till all of the voting precincts throughout the state will be closed and you the people will have selected your winner. What once was a fierce match which saw a slight increase in popularity for Mr. George Whip over Joe Weeks, has now turned into a dismal day for Mr. Whip and his campaign as word about his marital affairs and spousal abuse has surfaced. His wife also spoke about how Mr. Whip contributed to the suicidal death of their daughter a couple of months ago. Here is the clip of Mrs. Whip on our news cast earlier this afternoon." As they play the clip, the reporter looks at the monitor, fixes up her hair, pads down her face with make up again, and waits for the count down from the producer for her to come back in. She's a five foot six blond and has been in the business of doing Special Repots and Live Coverage for roughly two years, her and Melaney are great friends and often share stories with one another. "And in five, four, three, two---" The producer chanted. "And as you have just witnessed my fellow Floridians, the testimony of Mrs. Whip, the wife of Mr. George Whip. At this time his whole campaign has been rocked, but we have not been able to reach Mr. Whip for further comments on this story. After the commercial break we will give you the details to the original reporter who broke this story, and the woman within Mr. Whip's own campaign who helped her to get this story out. We will be back in a few." "And cut...", the producer said, "You have about three and a half minutes till you're back on the air." "What a sleaze ball this guy is, he beats on his wife and kills his child; this guy should be in jail." The reporter said under her breath as she pats herself down again, "and to think that I was planning on voting for this jerk."

AND THE
WINNER IS...

"Ladies and gentleman we are live here in Orlando, Florida, ready to announce the winner of this years District nineteen Florida State Senate Race. After a long day of counts and recounts, Florida has elected one of their next state senators. Yesterday we witnessed some devastating news from the estranged wife of Mr. George Whip. Her testimony could have been the deciding factor to this election. Without further due, we are primed to announce the winner of this particular District nineteen Florida Senate race.   And the winner is Mr. Joe Weeks with twenty thousand more votes than Mr. George Whip. Undoubtedly all of that last minute controversy reflected this election. A powerful win for Mr. Weeks who spent half of what Mr. Whip spent on marketing dollars for the campaign. We will try to speak with Mr. Weeks in a moment, as his camp begins to celebrate and pop the bottles for victory over Mr. George Whip."   "We will also try to get in contact with Mr. Whip as well; since that has been seemingly hard to do all day. We aren't even sure if he is going to deliver his final speech. Reporting live here at the camp of Mr. Joe Weeks, I am Michelle Steward, and I'll be back after these messages from our sponsors." "Wow! We won! We won!" My mother cheered, as she danced around the living room with joy. "I thought we just lost. The news just said that Joe Weeks has been elected as Senator." "No baby, we won, don't you see, Ms. Melany and I campaigned against Mr. Whip in the last hours and won." "You see, that's what I told you could happen. When us women come together against dirty men like him," Melany said to my mother as my father looked on from the kitchen. "It is by the grace of God that we kept another dirty politician out of office." My mother reeked with joy.

"Grace, yes, God, well I'm working on it." "Oh, you don't know Jesus!" Uh oh, here we go….. "I know Jesus, but I don't think I really know who Jesus is. You know, I've heard of him before. You get what I'm saying Sandra? I know him but I don't really know him. I guess what I'm saying is that I'm trying to build a relationship with him. It just seems so hard in this world of cut throat politics, backstabbing and rubber necking. I just would like to see more of Jesus in places like the capitol and I just don't know. Maybe in a couple of years Jesus and I would be best friends, but for now, it's best for me to kind of keep him at a distance. I believe that the opportunity for advancement would be better for me, if I could just keep religion out of my life at this time. Nothing wrong with Jesus and God or the Angels, I guess I'd rather just straddle the fence a little till I get to where I need to get to in this world."

My mother intervened, "Well, Melany, I appreciate you showing me that women can come together and help to at least shape one part of the world. But when God sent his only son Jesus, some thousands of years ago, he helped to change the whole world. Don't put God at a distance, he loves you, he cares for you more than any job or thing that you could ever acquire. I believe that the good Lord put us two together this day for me to share with you the goodness of his favor and love that he has towards you and all of his people. Please don't give up on God, because he'll never give up on you. And whether you realize it or not, you've already been promoted; you've been promoted with love from God for the gesture you did to fight evil. The word says those who do unto the least of them, do unto me. Now, that's not the exact scripture, so don't quote me on that. It's close though, it's close."

"Thank you so much Mrs. Lewis, I never really heard it said like that. I guess my butt needs to have a talk with God. I hope he still loves me after all I said." "Melany, he never stopped loving you, and he still loves Mr. Whip after all the wrong he's done. You see Melany, God makes us all to be beautiful, but it's sin that makes us ugly. You have a good night now Melany, and get in to a deep prayer with the one whom loves you the most." "Okay, I'll do that," Melany replied with a look of guilt and shame stretching across her light brown face. "What was that you said about being beautiful?" My mother paused, looked at my father, then swung back around and said to Melany, "God made us all to be beautiful, its sin that makes us out to be ugly. Therefore we are all beautifully ugly people." "Not me," my brother Joseph said. "Even you, Mr. Perfect, you are beautifully ugly too. So let me repeat myself," my mother grinned with a smile. "We are all beautifully ugly people no matter who we are or where we are from."

JOE WEEKS

"Hey baby."   "Hey Joe," Mrs.
Weeks wakes her husband up for a morning brew.
"So, what are the numbers like, babe?" Joe looked
on at her as if he was totally stunned by her
beauty, or maybe he is. They've been married for a
good twenty years now, and were married at
twenty-three and twenty-six with Joe being the
oldest. Gravity has done its number on Melinda
and Joe Weeks, but their vows of love may stand
the   test   of   time.
"Hey honey, can we not talk politics today? You
know the kids and I were thinking about going out
and fishing for some Bass. You're going to love it,
besides; it's about time you were able to take a
break   from   that   campaign."
"Now Melinda you know the game of politics, lib-
erals don't sleep till their occupying your town,
and even then they like to squat on everyone else's
stuff."   "I know, I know, but can we
just do something that the four of us could love.
You know Clyde is down from school and Cacey's
wanted to go fishing with you since last year. I

want my husband back, and they need their father." She finished adding the cream and sugars to their cups; she knows just how he likes it all the way down to the milligram of sugar that her husband enjoys in his cup of coffee. The two were made for each other, maybe even inseparable. "Well sweetie I have a meeting with my assistant in an hour, the meeting is only suppose to last about thirty minutes max." "You have been spending an awful amount of time with that assistant of yours, is everything ok," She looked away, not wanting to visualize anything that could come between their marriage. "Yes, he and I have been spending a lot of time together because we have a campaign to win," he said sarcastically. "But what's the point in running a campaign if you can't win the vote of your immediate family, now wouldn't that be hypocrisy to the third degree." "Listen Melanie, I'll be back in two hours, I love you. I'll do anything you and the kids want me to when I get back." He said with a political smile, not a smile which had an attachment of love and peace. "Ok honey, bye." She kissed him on his lower lip hoping that he could make a change for the future

"You're late boss." "I know, I had to get past the armed guard of a wife I have, you know how she gets to worrying and talking about how much time we haven't been spending with each other." "Tell me about it," his assistant looked on at him with a deep pleasure, knowing that the corruption of family is the key to the corruption of this county. "So tell me Joe, how long will you keep living the lie?" "What lie?" Joe fizzled around his pockets, unsure of what his assistant was referring to. "Now Joe, you know who I am, that daughter of yours that you've been making secret payments too, the money that you have hidden in that Swiss Account, that went untaxed. Don't you know that I know this, I have to know. Now is the time to prepare your wife for a potential media frenzy if anyone outside of these doors were to ever find out. You have done a wonderful job with the pay-off of the child's mother, but what if some wealthy banker or individual that does not like you; start to do some hardcore digging. Then, what will you do?" "Well, I don't know Zagan, help me, and tell me what to do. "He was flustered and confused. His campaign has stood on the idea that he has held good Christian standards and according to the latest polls, he seemed to win the most favor amongst conservative Christians. "I have already told you what you have to do Joseph Henry Weeks, lend your soul to the Prince of this world and all of this can go away in an instant." A Zagan motion for Joe to come forward, a blood sacrifice was needed to seal the deal of Joe's fate. "But I can't, I am a Christian,

you see I love God and Jesus is my Savior."
"You dare utter such a name in my presence, do you know that he can kill me. I am here to help you win this election, not him."
"I just can't, I can't sale my soul for man's glory. Yes I made some mistakes in the past, which I will have to deal with; I'll take it up my wife and my God. But to sale my soul for a few years in office, this I cannot do."
"Your decision is unfruitful; my master will not be pleased." He backed up a bit, eyes filled with the look of death, black as night they are, something so terrible, that no common man could defeat him.

Although he was a little spooked by Zagan's physical changes, he decided to make his final declaration in spite of, "Well, so be it. I would rather stand for righteousness, than to flirt with the pits of evil."
"You have already flirted with the forces of darkness Joe, and so far it's been a pretty good date."
"Perhaps, but at least I still have a chance for redemption while there is yet breath in my body. You on the other hand are cast to an eternal damnation." Zagan stood up, his lips were sealed. "That's what's wrong with you so called Christians, you flirt with evil, and then you want to judge when the date is no longer in your favor. My master and I know the bible backwards and forwards, there is nothing you can say that will change my allegiance."

"I'm sorry pal, you're just going to have to kill me, before I dare take such an oath to Satan, you never told me this was apart of the agreement." "Of course it was a part of the agreement, there is always a price to be paid. Even when that price is as simple as your soul, that's all he wants, you don't have to come out of pocket for what you already   own."
"That's just it; I'll be out of pocket with the one who made me. I can't pay that type of price. My eternal dwelling is based on my mortal decisions. For the last time, I respectfully decline."

"Hey baby, you made it back on time. I knew you'd be here for us. Are you okay?" Joe looked down at his watch and then upward to the sky.   "Yes honey,   I'm   ok.   I'm   just   fine."
"How did the meeting go Joe?" Curiosity brought her to question his demeanor.   "Let's just   say,   thank   God   for   second   chances, it is only because of him, which I can truly say I am blessed and highly favored. "Well Joe, whatever happened, I'm happy to see you here with your family."

READING GROUP GUIDE:

More Beautifully Ugly People has brought you the reader into the world of politics, and the secrets and back deals that take place; this is the third book in the series unlike the first two that proceeded. Beautifully Ugly People! And I am The Secret! focused heavily on the Lewis family and their issues, while More Beautifully Ugly People focused heavily on the flawed characteristics of George Whip and Joe Weeks. This may be the last book in the Beautifully Ugly People! Series which include the Lewis family, The next book to be released in the series will be Fat People! this does not have a scheduled release date yet.   I hope that this book encourages you to do the research as you choose the proper candidate this election year.

Discussion Questions:

1. Do you believe in the supernatural?

2. What is your opinion on demons? Based upon your opinion, do you feel that Christians can be

demonically possessed?

3. Do you believe that Sonya was justified in committing suicide?

4. What could anyone have done to help Sonya?

5. Do you believe that individuals who commit suicide have an after life in heaven?

5. "For he comes in with vanity, and departs in darkness, and his name shall be covered with darkness."-Ecclesiastes 6:4 What does this scripture mean to you, does it represent the overall theme of this book.

6. Why were Sandra and Joseph's relationship at such odds with each other?

7. George Whip mentioned his mater being the Price of Darkness, who exactly was he referring to when he said this?

8. Joe Weeks had an opportunity to sale his soul for a clean slate in life? Would you take this same deal if you had the chance?

9. What was Sandra Lewis's position with the George Whip Campaign?

10. What is the name of the reporter which first broke the story about George Whip's abuse and unfair pay practices?

ABOUT THE AUTHOR

Author Michael Beckford is a veteran in the publishing industry, having published his first book at eighteen years of age in 2004; he often consults others on their publishing dreams. More Beautifully Ugly People! is the sixth book to be published by the young Michael Beckford as he continues to inspire lives and work the mission which God has given him as a writer.

Acknowledgements

I want to thank everyone that has helped to make this Beautifully Ugly People! Series a success. It is because of you the reader that I am able to continue to lend my God given talents and be a voice for those who are unheard. I also acknowledge some of my closest friends for keeping me inspired even when I have been ready to give up and throw in the towel. There are so many of you, but I shall name a few...Royce Lovett, Antareo Johnson, Demetrius Wilkens, Ashley Williams, Maurice Hicks a.k.a. 'Uncle Reece, Elleanar

Harper, Rhema Soul, Barbara Joe Williams, Tremayne Moore, Tori Floyd, Montice Boss Writer Harmon, Victoria Christopher Murray, Reshonda Tate Billingsley, Demarco Speight, Shalanda Moore, Rev. Hall, Brandon Rittman, Somthin, Keheinde Singadore, Ismael Luxama, Darren Mason, Desmond Crayton, Willette White, Cheryl Jennings, Jadanis Avilus, Mahir Rutherford and my Facebook Family. I would also like to thank everyone in my immediate family, my church family, and anyone that has ever appreciated the work that I do. Thank you Mom and Dad, Latrice and my siblings, it is because of all of you, which makes me to be all of me. I love you.

PLEASE PLACE YOUR REVIEW OF THIS BOOK ON AMAZON.COM, BARNES & NOBLE.COM AND ANY OTHER FINE RETAILER. YOUR REVIEWS ARE ESSENTIAL FOR THE GROWTH AND SUCCESS OF ALL WRITERS. THANKS IN ADVANCE FOR THE ONE MINUTE OF YOUR TIME IT WILL TAKE TO WRITE A SIMPLE REVIEW. GOD BLESS YOU.

OTHER BOOK TITLES YOU MAY ENJOY BY MICHAEL D. BECKFORD

The Good Christian
The Bad Christian
The Christian
The Perfect Christian
FATHERHOOD
Mila's Big Day! (A Children's Book)

URBAN CLASSICS COLLECTION

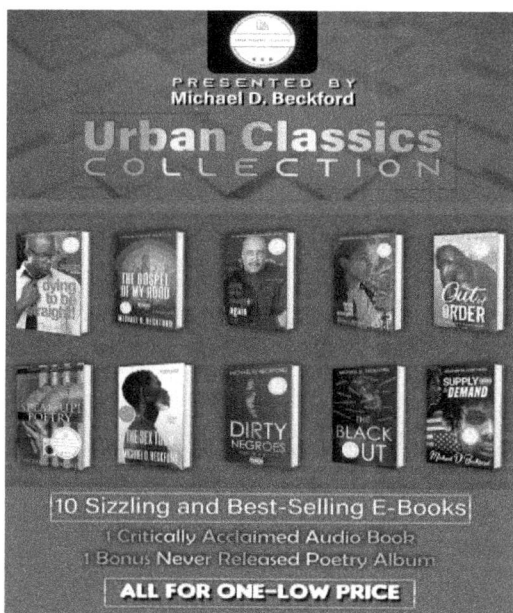

Get an instant $5 off This 10 E-Book and Audiobook URBAN CLASSICS COLLECTION **This 10 Ebook 1 Audio Book and 1 Poetry Album bundle is available Exclusively on Gumroad.com*** For **Only $19.99** with instant discount. Order

URBAN CLASSICS COLLECTION Now.